1001
Inspirational
Quotes
for
Entrepreneurs

Jack Burkhart

Copyright ©2000-2016 Jack Burkhart
Published by OpporTunaMedia, an imprint of
CordaNobeloMedia, printed by Createspace.com.
Publisher can be reached at
Publisher@CordaNobelo.com.

Library of Congress Cataloging-in-Publication Data:
for ordering information see back cover.

**Collect all 4 books in the "Inspirations for
Entrepreneurs" Series:**
"The Quotable Entrepreneur"
"Shake the Damned Tree!"
"Fortune Favors The Bold"
"1001 Inspirational Quotes for Entrepreneurs"

See also www.OpporTunaMedia.com

Acknowledgements

Thanks for everything to all the entrepreneurs I have worked with in Digital People, a large nonprofit for entrepreneurs. Also, to A. David Silver for his inspirational book "The Entrepreneurial Life," to Entrepreneurship Professors Dan Muzyka and Bill Bygrave and, most of all, to Hermann Hauser, Gentleman Entrepreneur.

Thanks also to my father and brother, Max and Torsten.

I have tried to attribute quotations as accurately as I can, and to acknowledge disparate sources. Any errors are honest errors and will be amended immediately you let me know!

Dedicated to entrepreneurs and futurepreneurs worldwide.....

Foreword

For an entrepreneur, Entrepreneurship is a more than way of life; it is a religion. There's just no other conceivable way to exist. Maybe for you, too?

As an entrepreneur in California's Silicon Valley, I had collected these quotes over the years to keep me cheerful. One Christmas, I decided to pull them all together into a book to give my entrepreneur friends for whom I couldn't afford to buy a present.

Years later, I went to visit an entrepreneur friend I had lost contact with and he still had a copy of this book on his bedside table, with coffee rings on it. He said he liked to read a few quotations every evening just before he went to sleep.

That's when I realized that other entrepreneurs like you might find these quotes useful. This is that book.

It was Nelson Mandela, once a prison inmate for 27 years, later President of South Africa and Noble Laureate, who said "The Struggle is my Life". If this rings true for you, then, as a fellow entrepreneur, I salute you!

Enjoy!
Jack Burkhart,
Palo Alto, California.

PS. For more inspirational quotes for entrepreneurs, check out the other books in the "Inspirations for Entrepreneurs" series. **If you think this book is useful for other entrepreneurs, then write a review on your online book retailer, email us your mailing address to publisher@cordanobelo.com and we will mail you another of the books in the series.**

PPS. Some of these quotes are historical, when entrepreneurs were presumably assumed to be exclusively male! Please let nobody be offended and please substitute "she" for "he", as appropriate.

6

One of the most important results you can bring
into the world is the you that you really want to
be
Robert Fritz

Better to have lived one day as a tiger than one thousand years as a sheep.
Tibetan saying.

There is one thing stronger than all the armies of the world, and that is an idea whose time has come.
Victor Hugo.

It is better to be free and poor than to have everything you want and have to do what someone tells you all the time.
Aesop.

The trick of society is to make you think it is the whole banana of life.
Laurence G. Boldt.
"Zen and the art of making a living."

Whatever you can do, or dream you can, begin it. Boldness has genius, power and magic in it.
Begin it now.
Wolfgang von Goethe.

Every great and commanding movement in the annals of the world is the triumph of enthusiasm. Nothing great was ever achieved without it.
Ralph Waldo Emerson.

Everyone has talent. What is rare is the courage to follow the talent to the dark place where it leads.
Erica Jong

Often the difference between a successful man and a failure is not one's better abilities or ideas, but the courage that one has to bet on his ideas, to take a calculated risk - and to act.
Maxwell Maltz

Nothing moves forward but by degrees. Each step forward, no matter how small, is one step less that has to be taken.
Brian Adams

Anyone who lives within his means suffers from a lack of imagination.
Lionel Stander.

Victory belongs to the most persevering.
Napoleon.

Procrastination is the thief of time.
Edward Young.

The shortest way to do many things is to do only
one thing at once.
Samuel Smiles

Most people can do extraordinary things if they
have the confidence or take the risks. Yet most
people don't. They sit in front of the TV and treat
life as if it goes on forever.
Philip Adamsin from Charles Banfe's
"Entrepreneur, From Zero to Hero"

The difficult things of the world must once have
been easy; the great things must once have been
small...A thousand mile journey begins with one
step.
Lao-Tse.

Don't be afraid to take a big step if one is
indicated. You can't cross a chasm in two small
jumps.
David Lloyd George.

Some men see things as they are and say "why?"
I dream things that never were and say "why
not?"
Robert Kennedy

The block of granite which was an obstacle in the
pathway of the weak became a stepping stone in
the pathway of the strong.
Thomas Carlyle.

Good ideas and innovations must be driven into
existence by courageous patience.
Admiral Rickover.

The secret of success is making your vocation
your vacation.
Mark Twain.

Our doubts are traitors, and make us lose the
good we oft might win by fearing to attempt.
William Shakespeare

Better to plow a crooked furrow than not plow
one at all.

A good plan violently executed right now is far better than a perfect plan executed next week.
General George Patton.

If a man does not work passionately (even furiously) at being the best in the world at what he does, he fails his talent, his destiny and his God.
George Louis.

Go confidently in the direction of your dream! Live the life you've imagined.
Henry David Thoreau.

It's a funny thing about life; if you refuse to accept anything but the best you very often get it.
W. Somerset Maugham.

They can because they think they can.
Virgil.

Every day sends to their graves obscure men whom timidity prevented them from making a first effort.
Sydney Smith

There is only one success - to be able to spend your life in your own way.
Christopher Morley

Until you try you don't know what you can't do.
Henry James.

It is not the critic that counts; not the man who points out how the strong man stumbled or where the doer of deeds could have done them better. The credit belongs to the man who is actually in the arena; whose face is marred by dust and sweat and blood; who strives valiantly; who errs, and come short again and again, because there is no effort without error and shortcomings, who does actually try to do the deed; who knows the great enthusiasm, the great devotion, and spends himself in a worthy cause; who, at the worst, if he fails, at least fails while daring greatly. Far better it is to dare mighty things, to win glorious triumphs even though checkered by failure, than to rank with those poor spirits who neither enjoy nor suffer much because they live in the gray twilight that know neither victory nor defeat.
Theodore Roosevelt.

Nothing in the world can take the place of persistence. Talent will not; nothing is more common than unsuccessful men with talent. Genius will not; unrewarded genius is almost a proverb. Education alone will not; the world is full of educated derelicts. Persistence and determination alone are omnipotent.
Calvin Coolidge.

To be what we are, and to become what we are capable of becoming, is the only end of life.
Robert Louis Stevenson.

The great aim of education is not knowledge but action.
Herbert Spencer.

Emptiness is a symptom that you are not living creatively. You either have no goal that is important enough to you, or you are not using your talents and efforts in striving towards an important goal.
Maxwell Maltz

Never give in.
Never give in.
Never give in
Winston Churchill.

Take your dream and attach it to a star.
Guru RHH

The truth is that all of us attain the greatest success and happiness possible in this life whenever we use our native capacities to their greatest extent.
Dr. Blanton.

While one person hesitates because he feels inferior, the other is busy making mistakes and becoming superior.
Henry C. Link.

Nothing would be done at all if a man waited until he could do it so well that no-one could find fault with it.
Cardinal Newman.

The great French Marshal Lyautey once asked his gardener to plant a tree. The gardener objected that the tree was slow growing and would not reach maturity for 100 years. The marshal replied: 'in that case, there is no time to lose; plant it this afternoon.'
John F. Kennedy.

Men stumble over the truth from time to time, but most pick themselves up and hurry off as if nothing had happened.
Sir Winston Churchill.

Failure is often the line of least persistence.
Zig Ziglar.

Action springs not from thought but from a
readiness for responsibility.
Dietrich Bonhoeffer.

The greatest pleasure in life
is doing what people
say you cannot do.
Walter Bagehot.

There is no heavier burden than a great
potential.
Charlie Brown

Business should be fun...Fun is a powerful motive
for most of our activities and should be a direct
path to our livelihood. We should not relegate it
to something we buy after work with money we
earn.
Michael Phillips.

Most men would feel insulted if it were proposed
to employ them in throwing stones over a wall,
and then throwing them back merely that they
might earn their wages. But many are no more
worthily employed now.
Henry David Thoreau.

Man cannot discover new oceans until he has the courage to lose sight of the shore.

A boat is safe in the harbor. But that is not what boats are for.

If you do what you've always done, you'll get what you've always gotten.

Winning starts with beginning.
Robert Schuller.

He who has begun his task has half done it.
Horace.

Boy, I've got a vision and the rest of the world wears bifocals.
Butch Cassidy

Whatever the mind of man can conceive and believe, it can achieve.
Napoleon Hill.

Search for the hero inside yourself, search for the secrets you hide.
Search for the hero inside yourself, until you find the key to your life.
Advertizement for Renault cars.

Entrepreneur: one who operates, organizes, or assumes the risks for a business venture.

The best ideas come as jokes.
Make your thinking as funny as possible.
David Ogilvy

Be daring. Be first. Be different.
Anita Roddick
founder of 'The Body Shop'.

One idea can change your future
Roger Shoshana

Dream big!

Most men lead lives of quiet desperation.
Thoreau

The reasonable man adapts himself to the world;
the unreasonable man persists in trying to adapt
the world to himself. Therefore all progress
depends on the unreasonable man.
George Bernard Shaw.

The man with a new idea is a crank, until the
idea succeeds.
Mark Twain

I think if you are stuck in a rut today, it's
because you got comfortable there.

As he thinketh in his heart, so is he.
Proverbs 23:7

We are what we think.
All that we are arises
With our thoughts.
With our thoughts,
We make our world.
Buddha.

Only in men's imagination does every truth find
an effective and undeniable existence.
Imagination, not invention, is the supreme
master of art, as in life.
Joseph Conrad.

[There is a] quality of supreme confidence
attached to winners.
Godfrey Golzen.

We are what we imagine ourselves to be.
Once you have decided what you want, the rest
is easy.

If we do not hold the possibility in our
imagination, then it is by definition impossible.

If you want to be happy, find something you love
doing so much that you would do it for free. Then
do it so well that people will pay you to do it for
them!

Every man-made thing, however small, started in someone's imagination.

Discover what talents of yours are never being exploited.
Godfrey Golzen.

Most of us abandoned the idea
of a life full of adventure and travel
sometime between puberty
and our first job.
Tim Cahill.

Tell a man he is brave and you help him to become so.
Thomas Carlyle.

The way we choose to live is an expression of our purpose.

Your goals must be emotionally consistent with how you see yourself.
David Krueger.

Nothing is enough for the man for whom enough is too little.
Epicurus.

Their essential drive is to make real the things they imagine could be.

If security no longer comes from being employed, then it must come from being employable.
Rosabeth Moss Kanter,
Harvard Business School.

The purpose of a job or career change should be that of seeking greater self-fulfillment.

If you want to rock the boat, don't go to sea with a load of old age pensioners.
Godfrey Golzen.

It's not the early bird that catches the worm, but the bird who recognizes the worm.

He who believes is strong; he who doubts is weak. Strong convictions precede great actions.
J.F. Clarke.

They lusted for power to do it right.
Harvard Business School students
Charles Banfe
"Entrepreneur: From Zero to Hero"

Action is eloquence.
William Shakespeare.

He's a-way way out there in the blue, riding on a
shoeshine and a smile.
Arthur Miller,
"Death of a Salesman."

Nothing was more frustrating than being
dependent on someone else for the opportunity
to succeed.
Edwin Land,
founder of Polaroid Corporation.

If you wanted to change the world,
of course you'd have to work all night.
Frank Rose,
Author of "West of Eden"
(history of Apple Computer)

Entrepreneurs have tended to be young men
from the middle class, who grew up without
fathers, got professional degrees but did not use
them, and had strong mothers.
A. David Silver.
"The Entrepreneurial Life"

The Only Dumb Question is the Question You
Don't Ask.
Sign on high school science lab wall.

The majority of people in the world have
inferiority complexes.
Ron Holland.

Dawn does not come twice to awaken the man.
Arab proverb.

He was going to do something. If only he knew
what.
Unknown

There can be no doubt that creativity is the most
important human resource of all.
Edward de Bono.

Instead they view self-employment as a workable
vehicle for achieving the control and flexibility
that eluded them in the corporate career track.
Amy Saltzmann,
"Downshifting"

To succeed you have to believe in something with
such a passion that it becomes a reality.
Anita Roddick,
founder of "The Body Shop"

Success comes not from specialization but from
being the best in a valuable combination of fields
Nolan Bushnell.

Building a successful business always takes
longer than the entrepreneur expects.
Warren Avis.

He has achieved success who has lived well,
laughed often and loved much.
Bessie Anderson Stanley
Brown Book magazine 1904.

I always wanted to .... but never got the
opportunity.
"Thelma & Louise."

A salesman is got to dream, boy. It comes with
the territory.
Arthur Miller,
"Death of a Salesman."

Since I really believe in what I'm selling, I don't
look at it as selling. It's more akin to missionary
work.
Anon

All things are difficult before they are easy.
John Norley.

Enthusiasm is the greatest vehicle of persuasion.
Sweat Morden

Ah, for a chance of greatness...
Anon

Several successful entrepreneurs had gone
through several start-ups, many of them failures,
prior to creating a "winner."
Karl Vesper.

Your knowledge and experience are unlike those
of anyone else in the world.
No-one looks at things quite the way you do.
Dan Poynton.

In the end, we are the sum-total of our
actions...Day by day we write our own destiny;
for inexorably...we become what we do.
Madame Chiang Kai-Shek.

Once an entrepreneur loses touch with his sense
of adventure, he joins hands with business
suicide.
Victor Kiam,
Remington.

Each of us houses two persons:
The me I am today, and
The me I'm going to be.
Denis Waitley.

When you go for something, don't come back 'til
you get it.
W. Clement Stone.

The only person you have to please is yourself.
Warden Henry
"Toughing it out in Harvard."

I am risking my life for it...and my reason has
half-foundered because of it...that's all right.
Vincent Van Gogh.

That it will never come again is what makes life
so sweet.
Emily Dickinson.

We were resolved to try a fundamentally different
principle.
Wright Brothers.

"Eureka!" (Greek for "I have found it") is the motto of the State of California.

Crisis is an opportunity riding a dangerous wind.
Chinese saying.

My motto is simple: if it ain't fun, don't do it!
Sam Zell.

Imagination rules the world.
Napoleon Bonaparte

One of the real problems we have with satisfying the consumer today is an absence of new products.
Journal of Product Innovation Management.

Whenever you see a successful business, someone once made a courageous decision.
Peter Drucker.

The people who get on in the world are the people who get up and look for the circumstances they want and, if they can't find them, make them.
George Bernard Shaw

Eventually [he] became convinced that the only person with the commitment to market the idea was himself.
Ron Hickman,
inventor of Black & Decker's "Workmate"
(portable workbench)

The future ain't what it used to be.
Apocryphal

All men are created equal. But who wants to be equal?
Nike ad 1995

To be good is not enough when you dream of being great.
NY School of Arts poster.

Shake the tree!
Anon

[Believe in] the power of one mind to change the universe.
Unknown

Live extraordinary lives.
"Dead Poets' Society"'

Innovation is the central issue in economic prosperity.
Michael Porter,
Harvard Business School.

And the trouble is, if you don't risk anything, you risk even more.
Erica Jong.

Imagination is the highest kite you can fly.
Lauren Bacall

If you can dream it, do it.
Walt Disney

It doesn't matter what the others say. You can go your own way...
Chris Rea

Another word for creativity is courage.
George Prince,
Founder, Synectics
It's better to be a pirate than join the navy.
Steve Jobs

If you're going to do a project, make it a big one, because a small one is just as much work.
Unknown

Shoot me, I'm going to do it anyway.
A. David Silver

The rapture, the glory and the glamour of the "very beginning."
Gertrude Bacon

Find a need and fill it!
Kaiser Sand & Gravel Co.

Entrepreneurship is a golden glitter by which the rest hope to join the rich.
J. Mancuso,
"Fun & Guts: the entrepreneur's philosophy."

Two roads diverged in a wood, and I
...I took the one less traveled by.
And that has made all the difference.
Robert Frost

Life's battles don't always go to the stronger or faster man.

But sooner or later the man who wins is the man
who thinks he can.
Napoleon Hill

What do you care what others think?
Richard Feynman

Desperation is the mother of invention.
A. David Silver.

Be a doer not a stewer.

Laziness is the mother of invention.
Thomas Alva Edison.

If necessity is the mother of invention, then discontent is the mother of entrepreneurship.
Charles Banfe,
Author, "Entrepreneur: From Zero to Hero."

Invention is the mother of necessity.

No one is paid to sit around being capable of achievement.
Edward de Bono

Better to burn out than it is to rot.
(Hey, hey, my, my, Rock & Roll will never die).
'60s rock song

Suck the marrow out of life.
"Dead Poets' Society."

Control your destiny or someone else will.
Jack Welch,
Former CEO, GE.

Many people have a desire to change their life situation.
Few people take action to do so.
"The Practice of Entrepreneurship"
International Labor Organization.

Invent it! Grow it! Sell it!

Our lives are creative acts.
"First find your hilltop."

It's very hard to be who we are because it doesn't seem to be what anyone wants.
Warren Bennis
Opportunity is the source of innovation.

Whatever you can do, or dream you can do, begin it!
Boldness has genius, power and magic in it.
Wolfgang von Goethe.

Boldness be my guide.
Title of book by a WWII concentration camp escapee

I think that never in my life have I experienced so much excitement, fun and commitment as

43

during this time working in my firm. It is
impossible to imagine that working for another
company could be so rewarding.
Interview with entrepreneur.

Just because I've never seen one doesn't mean I
can't imagine one.
(picture of rainbow)
from a poster for an organization for the blind.

Do the thing and you shall have the power.
Ralph Waldo Emerson

Believe in the American dream: that if you
wanted something badly enough and devoted
your heart and soul to it, you would ultimately
succeed.
Erich Segal.

People occupying frontier positions, exposed to
constant attack, achieve a more brilliant
development than their neighbors in more
sheltered positions.
Arnold Toynbee.

Creative persons are often perceived as oddballs and by fellow workers as not good "team players."
Charles Banfe,
"Entrepreneur: From Zero to Hero"

Bell's initial patent application for the telephone was the single most valuable patent ever granted.
P.C. Wensberg.
"Land's Polaroid"

Three-fourths of those things upon which action in war must be calculated are hidden more or less in the clouds of great uncertainty.
Clausewitz.

Companies with fewer than 100 employees created 80% of net new jobs in the US economy during the 1970s.

I went for the jugular question.
Nobel Laureate.

The obscure we see eventually. The completely apparent takes longer.
Edward R. Murrow,
Broadcaster.

There were all kinds of things I was afraid of at first but, by acting as if I was not afraid, I gradually ceased to be afraid.
Theodore Roosevelt.

In the land of the blind, the one-eyed man is king.
H.G. Wells.

Leap and the net will appear.

[Eli Whitney:] his ability to provide what the nation wanted at a time when it most wanted it was to characterize Whitney's career.

We are all salesmen, every day of our lives.
Charles Schwab.

To insist on one's place in the scheme of things and live up to that place.
Robert Fulghum,
"Uh-Oh"

Luck lies at the intersection of preparation and opportunity.
Denis Waitley.

Are you ready to abandon any agenda to pursue opportunity?
Fuqua.

Expect a miracle.

[People] now approach entrepreneurship primarily as a lifestyle decision...a more reasonable way to conduct their careers and live their lives.
Amy Saltzmann,
"Downshifting"

Entrepreneurs:
 the only people who work 80 hour weeks
 to avoid working 40 hour weeks.

He that will not apply new remedies must expect new evils, for time is the greatest innovator.
Francis Bacon,
"On Innovation"

Don't enjoy being poor.
Warren Avis.

Most entrepreneurs seem to be misfits who need to create their own environment.
Manfred Kets De Vries.

You have an individuality...cling to it, cherish it, develop it.
Dale Carnegie.

Start with a low overhead, and be willing to do everything yourself.
Liz Claiborne.

The world makes way for the person who knows where he is going.
Ralph Waldo Emerson.

Destiny is not a matter of chance, it is a matter of choice.

The creative mind is a muscle. Develop it by pumping ideas. There should always be a goofy time for asking, "I wonder why?"

Too many men are working in jobs they do not like.
"Sweat Morden"

He thought only that he wished to have joy and reason and meaning in life - and that none had been offered to him anywhere.
Ayn Rand,
"Fountainhead"

You can do it.

Imagination is more important than knowledge.
Albert Einstein.

People need heroes. And Americans, more than
any other people, have made heroes out of
inventors.
Smithsonian book of invention.

The secret in happiness is not in doing what one
likes, but in liking what one does.
James M. Barrie.

Be the best you can be.
US Army.

The pride you take in your product or service will
give you the strength to deal with rejection in a
positive manner.
Victor Kiam,
Remington.

He fills the room with his ideas...[he is]
challenging, stimulating, exciting...
"The Charismatic Leader"
Jay A. Conger.

Once an opportunity is generally known, it is
pretty well gone.
George Gilder.

We are continually faced by great opportunities
brilliantly disguised as insoluble problems.

If you ain't got no prospects, you ain't got no
prospects.
(from a salesperson's guide to selling).

A man is not what he thinks he is
but what he thinks, he is.
Ralph Waldo Emerson.

A man's reach should exceed his grasp, or what's
a heaven for?
Robert Browning.

They would succeed. They would overcome nature. They would be ready. And ready, to the inventor, meant ready to walk upon a broader stage.
(of Edwin Land from "Land's Polaroid")
P.C. Wensberg.

Any one thing you want you can have, as long as you know what it is and subordinate everything else to it.
Robert Collier,
"The Book of Life."

Great products have a soul.
William Davidow.

All the great inventions of the past had their origin in this kind of inquisitive mind.

It's your work in life that is the ultimate seduction.
Pablo Picasso.

Does your work pass the "cocktail party test"?

Creativity has to do with the ability to question.
Michael Ray & Rochelle Myers.
"Creativity in Business"

Lead, follow, or get out of the way!

All cases are unique, and very similar to others.
T.S.Eliot.

I came to the conclusion that the gift of fantasy
has meant more to me than my talent of
absorbing positive knowledge.
Albert Einstein.

No man can have self-confidence if not convinced
in his own mind that he is qualified to perform
the job he is assigned.

Live extraordinary lives.
"Dead Poets' Society"

Take time for sunsets and flowers.
Denis Waitley.

It is change which always provides opportunity
for the new and different.
Peter Drucker.

Never do anything you don't enjoy, and try to do
it better than anyone else.

55

I could have quit many times –
given up, because it is not great art in life to be
poor and hungry, and that's what I was.
Erskine Caldwell.

[James Goldsmith (billionaire) was a driven
man:the sense of having to prove to others that
he was better than they were; to get his own
back on those who had jeered at him; he was
already an outsider and would remain so always;
drawn to other misfits like himself, always
against the establishment, whatever than meant
at the time.
"Billionaire"
Ivan Fallon.

A product is only worth what somebody is willing
to pay for it.
Warren Avis.

He who rides a tiger cannot dismount.
Chinese proverb.

The greater part of mankind have no great
character at all, have little that distinguishes
them from others...
Samuel Johnson.

Colonel Harlan Sanders lived in his car for two years peddling and demonstrating a Kentucky Fried Chicken recipe and breaded chicken product.
Charles Banfe,
"Entrepreneur: from Zero to Hero"

Freedom "to be able to tell anybody to go to hell"
Karl Vesper.

When your plan appears - act upon it. You will know it.
Sweat Morden.

You are much more likely to get rich from hard work than from a lucky win.
Aesop.

There are two great tragedies in life: never to have had a dream to strive for, ever to have fully reached it.
Denis Waitley.

Little ideas provoke little comment. [so think big!]

So easy it seemed
Once found which yet unfound most would have
thought impossible.
Milton,
"Paradise Lost."

All of a sudden I realized that I was at least as
smart and as good as the people I was working
for. That was the major difference in my career.
From then on, I just started to grow...

Hope is a good breakfast but a bad supper.
Roger Bacon.

Survey large fields but cultivate small ones.
H. C. Kimble.

As a man thinketh, so shall he be.
Proverb.

If a company is promising enough, the capital for it can be found.
Karl Vesper.

The mass of men lead lives of quiet desperation.
Thoreau.

The quick and the dead: be quick or you're dead.

The vast majority of any rejections you receive
have nothing to do with you, your firm or the
service you have identified. The automatic
response of mankind to any new suggestion,
change, request, or idea is "no".
Richard Conner,
"Getting New Clients."

Invent it, grow it, sell it!

Why is it I get my best ideas in the morning while
I am shaving?
Albert Einstein.

Every great work of art comes from a clear
perception on the part of its creator which
resonates within a clear perception on the part of
the audience.
Michael Ray & Rochelle Myers,
"Creativity in Business"

Carpe diem!
Seize the day!
"Dead Poets' Society"

It is better to go foaming over the precipice than waste your life in sandy deltas.

All growth depends on activity.
Calvin Coolidge.

In business there are
Those who make it happen,
Those who watch it happen,
and
Those who ask "what's happening?"
Michael Maccoby,
"The Leader"

When you continually feel in danger of losing your job because of organizational reshufflings and mergers, the relative risks of self-employment are minimal.
Amy Saltzmann,
"Downshifting"

Innovations in consumer goods must reinforce
social values. Inventions that need promotion
least are those whose social utility seems
obvious. Inventions that need promotion are
those whose pre-existing demand is either weak
or problematic. Much contemporary gadgetry falls
into this category.
Peter Drucker.

I've always learned that it's always better
to have a small percentage of a big business
than a hundred percent of nothing.
Warren Avis.

A man bent on implementing a strong and
unconventional vision cannot help to antagonize
powerful others who might hold different views.

Leaders can become prisoners of their own
psychic theater.
Manfred Kets De Vries.

Customers: they're not stupid, they're just
uninformed.

The consumer is not stupid, she's your wife.
David Ogilvy.

It was certainly better to imagine myself becoming famous than maturing into a stifled academic who had never risked a thought.
Watson,
"The Double Helix"

When you fail to plan, you plan to fail.

Every great organization is the "lengthened shadow of one person".

People are made great by the causes they serve.

I am a man who does not exist for others.
(Of Howard Roark)
Ayn Rand,
"The Fountainhead."

Grasp the nettle tightly, not lightly.
Aesop.

There are only a few men in all of history, who have changed the lives of other men, as much as the inventor of the first useful electric light. (= Edison.)

Go for the big P (the big problems).
A. David Silver.

....something commensurate to his capacity for
wonder.
F. Scott Fitzgerald.

One idea can change your future.
Roger Shoshana.

Every day in every way I'm getting better and
better.
Emile Coué.

For the first time, business leaders began to
share the limelight with great political leaders.
"The Charismatic Leader"
Jay A. Conger.

In listing the characteristics of creativity:
Wonder, first of all.
Regis McKenna.

The entrepreneur's nature: as much mischievous
as attention-seeking.
David Robinson,
"The Naked Entrepreneur"

Genius is the ability to reduce the complicated to
the simple.
C.W. Ceron.

I left my job because I wanted the chance to do
things the way I knew they should be done.
from Charles Banfe,
"Entrepreneur: From Zero to Hero."

If you never experiment, you can never improve.

Authority flows from the one who knows.
Proverb.

73% of product innovations come from market
needs, whereas 27% come from technological
opportunities.
Urban & Hauser,
'Design & Marketing of New Products"

Stay on the steep portion of the learning curve.
Michael Ray & Rochelle Myers

"Creativity in Business"

If you see in any given situation only what
everybody else can see, you can be said to be so
much a representative of your culture that you
are a victim of it.
S. I. Hayakawa.
former Senator.

Make a difference.

Ambition was the motive force and he was
powerless to resist it.
Sir Winston Churchill,
"Savrola"

Choose an idea-sensitive area with lots of
potential.
Edward de Bono.

Nothing great was ever achieved without
enthusiasm.
Ralph Waldo Emerson.

You should start doing great things right
away...Not trying to save yourself for the great
day when you become famous, but just do the
best you can each day.
Charles Schulz,
"Peanuts" cartoonist.

If I want do something, I won't accept failure.
Because until I do something I haven't failed.
Bob Hoskins.
Passion persuades, and by God, I was passionate
about what I was selling.
Anita Roddick,
founder of "The Body Shop"

Over the years I have come to realize that my
greatest weakness is my unwillingness
sometimes to stay with a job as long as
necessary to achieve optimum results.
Warren Avis.

[The entrepreneur is often a] constructive
narcissist.
Manfred Kets de Vries.

Create an anomaly sieve.
H. Skip Weitzen,
"Hypergrowth"

I think the person who takes a job in order to live
- that is to say, (just) for the money - has turned
himself into a slave.
Joseph Campbell.

Everyone wants success. Not everyone is willing
to work for it.

Nothing is ours but time.
Seneca.

When I decided to start for myself it was because
I felt that no-one else would pay me as well as
W.R.Morris.
William Morris, car manufacturer.

Many a cold-blooded banker has been swayed by
the confidence, belief and enthusiasm he sees in
a would-be borrower.
"Sweat Morden"

Do it now!

Successful people believe in their own worth, even when they have nothing but a dream to hang onto. Why? Because their own self-worth is stronger than the rejection or acceptance of their idea by others.
Denis Waitley.

[Inventors have] a belief of being part of something greater than themselves.
Roger Shoshana.

These leaders feel outraged by wasted human potential in bureaucracies that grind people down.
"The Leader,"
Michael Maccoby.

The essence of charisma is showing your commitment to an idea or goal.
Roger Ailes.

Failure is the opportunity to begin again more intelligently.
Henry Ford.

Allow your imagination to dance.

Money is the fuel.
Charles Banfe,
"Entrepreneur: From Zero to Hero."

[The creative drive of inventive scientists:] I find
the first event is an urge to make a significant
contribution that can be tangibly embodied in a
product or process.
Edwin Land,
founder of Polaroid Corporation.

It's not the facts that are important but what you
do with them and how you interpret them.

In marketing, I would rather be significantly
different than just a little bit better.
William Davidow.

To successfully penetrate a targeted niche you
must offer "silver bullets." These are the
solutions to the "hot-button needs."
Richard Conner,
"Getting New Clients."

Never accept the status quo.

Recognition of demand is a more frequent factor in successful innovation than recognition of technological potential.
Professor Marquis,
MIT R&D Management Group.

Do nothing without enthusiasm.

Creativity's not talking, it's the ability to listen.
Michael Ray & Rochelle Myers.
"Creativity in Business"

To thine own self be true, and it must follow, as the night the day, thou canst not then be false to any man.
Shakespeare.

If I had a great deal of money I would....[fill in the blank]
Denis Waitley.

You've got to be willing to work hard enough to prove your ideas will work. People will be interested in you after you've proved your ideas. Not before.
Xavier Roberts.
inventor of the "Cabbage Patch Dolls"

I went to the woods because I wished to live deliberately, to front only the essential facts of life, and see if I could not learn what it had to teach, and not, when I came to die, discover that I had not lived.
Henry David Thoreau.

A successful entrepreneur has to be prepared to lose everything and start all over again.
Warren Avis.

When everyone zigs, you should zag.
Shirley Polykoff,
copywriter.

Too many people spend money they haven't earned, to buy things they don't want, to impress people they don't like.
Will Rogers.

The losers in life are those who want to look like
earn like,
dress like,
take time off like,
travel like,
own like,
retire like, and
be somebody else.
Denis Waitley.

I wouldn't work this hard for anyone else but me.
Advertisement for American Express card.

I have but one merit, that of never despairing.
Marshall Foch.

Do you understand what it's like to work forty
years of your goddamn life for one goal? Do you
understand what it means to sacrifice your youth
for nothing? The first lesson is how to enjoy life.
To take satisfaction from what [you've] already
accomplished.
Erich Segal,
"The Class."

To be famous is a great thing. I have always
wanted to be great - so good that the people who
knew what I was doing would understand it.
Ray Charles.

"I know it will work."
"Yeah? Well, you don't run things around here."
Ayn Rand.
"Fountainhead"

I have so much to do and life is so short that I
must work fast.
Thomas Alva Edison.

74

90 hours a week and loving it!
Apple Macintosh team T-shirt

When the going gets tough, the tough get going.

It takes less work to succeed than to fail.
W. Clement Stone.

It's not an easy life. Nothing worthwhile is ever
easy. If David had slain a dwarf instead of a
giant, who would have cared?
Victor Kiam.

I will study and prepare myself and some day my
chance will come.
Abraham Lincoln

Work and hope. But never hope more than you
work.
Beryl Markham.
"West with the night."

Try not.
Do or do not.
There is no try.
Yoda,
"Star Wars."

Do it! Don't let life and opportunity pass you by!
Dan Muzyka
Professor of Entrepreneurship

If I'm not for myself, who will be for me?
If not this way, how?
If not now, when?
Primo Levi
"Song of the Partisan"

If I'm not for myself, who will be for me?
If I am only for myself, what am I?
If not now, when?
Rabbi Hillel.

When you go for something don't come back until
you get it.
W. Clement Stone

Do one thing at a time, but do it, and now!
Fred Smith,
Founder, Federal Express.

[The secret of success is] to be afraid last.
Napoleon.

A fortune is only an idea acted upon.
David Schwartz.

A man is what he thinks about all day long.
Ralph Waldo Emerson.

To succeed you have to believe in something with such a passion that it becomes a necessity.
Anita Roddick,
founder of "The Body Shop."

First and foremost, an entrepreneur is a dreamer.
Charles Banfe.
Author, "Entrepreneur: from Zero to Hero."

What will I do with my creativity? [Do something worthy]
A. David Silver.

Most [people] will continue to wonder...dream...and wish.
W. Clement Stone.

To live a creative life, we must lose our fear of being wrong.
Joseph Chilton Pearce.

Every time we say "Let there be!" in any form, something happens.
Stella Terrill Mann.

Go confidently in the direction of your dreams!
Live the life you've imagined. As you simplify
your life, the laws of the universe will be simpler.
Henry David Thoreau.

Undoubtedly we become what we envisage.
Claude M. Bristol

Every time you don't follow your inner guidance,
you feel a loss of energy, loss of power, a sense
of spiritual deadness.
Shakti Gawain.

To know what you prefer instead of humbly
saying "Amen" to what the world tells you you
ought to prefer, is to have kept your soul alive.
Robert Louis Stevenson.
Genuine beginnings begin within us, even when
they are brought to our attention by external
opportunities.
William Bridges.

What doesn't kill me makes me stronger.
Albert Camus.

The solitary tree, if it grows at all, grows more
strongly.
Winston Churchill.

It don't mean a thing if it ain't got that swing.
Duke Ellington & Irving Mills.

Your desire is your prayer. Picture the fulfillment
of your desire now and feel its reality and you will
experience the joy of the answered prayer.
Dr. Joseph Murphy .

The world of reality has its limits; the world of
imagination is boundless.
Jean-Jacques Rousseau.

Man can learn nothing except going from the
known to the unknown.
Claude Bernard.

Trust that still, small voice that says, "This might
work and I'll try it."
Diane Marie Child .

Dare to be the poet of your life's song.
Laurence G. Boldt.
"Zen and the art of making a living"

Only those who will risk going too far can
possibly find out how far one can go.
T.S. Eliot.

Life shrinks or expands in proportion to one's
courage.
Anais Nin.
Just do it.
Nike.

Because one day you'll die.
Levi jeans ad.

Twenty years from now you will be more
disappointed by the things that you didn't do
than by the ones you did do. So throw off the
bowlines. Sail away from the safe harbor. Catch
the trade winds in your sails. Explore. Dream.
Discover.
Mark Twain

There is a tide in the affairs of men
Which, taken at the flood, leads on to fortune;
Omitted, all the voyage of their life
Is bound in shallows and in miseries.
On such a full sea we are now afloat;
And we must take the current when it serves,
Or lose the ventures before us.
William Shakespeare

Genius is 1% inspiration, and 99% perspiration.
Thomas Edison

Being an entrepreneur is a lot like playing poker:
you can fold, limp in, or go for it.
Yasmine Mustafa

The future belongs to those who believe in the
beauty of their dreams.
Eleanor Roosevelt

They never told me I couldn't.
Tom Dempsey

I have learned over the years when one's mind is made up, this diminishes fear; knowing what must be done does away with fear.
Rosa Parks

Entrepreneurship is the last refuge of the trouble-making individual.
Natalie Clifford Barney

I have not failed. I've just found 10,000 ways that won't work.
Thomas Edison

Formal education will make you a living; self-education will make you a fortune.
Jim Rohn

The most valuable thing you can make is a mistake – you can't learn anything from being perfect.
Adam Osborne

A man must be big enough to admit his mistakes, smart enough to profit from them, and strong enough to correct them.
John C. Maxwell

Listening is the most powerful weapon after self-belief and persistence you can bring into play as an entrepreneur.
Felix Dennis

Our business in life is not to get ahead of others, but to get ahead of ourselves.
E. Joseph Cossman

Logic will get you from A to B. Imagination will take you everywhere. Albert Einstein

You can't ask customers what they want and then try to give that to them. By the time you get it built, they'll want something new.
Steve Jobs
Live out of your imagination instead of out of your memory.
Fortune Cookie

Success is liking yourself, liking what you do, and liking how you do it.
Maya Angelou

What is robbing a bank compared with founding a bank?
Bertold Brecht

If you are seeking creative ideas, go out walking.
Angels whisper to a man when he goes for a
walk.
Raymond Inman

Success is walking from failure to failure with no
loss of enthusiasm.
Winston Churchill

A man's worth is no greater than the worth of his
ambitions.
Marcus Aurelius

If you cannot do great things, do small things in
a great way.
Napoleon Hill

I don't know the key to success, but the key to
failure is trying to please everybody.
Bill Cosby

There comes a time in a man's life when to get
where he has to go – if there are no doors or
windows – he walks through a wall.
Bernard Malmud

Tell everyone what you want to do and someone will want to help you do it.
W. Clement Stone

Success is not in what you have, but who you are.
Bo Bennett

You're gonna lose some ballgames and you're gonna win some ballgames and that's about it.
Sparky Anderson

Coming together is a beginning; keeping together is progress; working together is success.
Henry Ford

Great achievement is usually born of great sacrifice, and is never the result of selfishness.
Napoleon Hill

Try not to be a man of success, but rather try to become a man of value. Albert Einstein

The best way to predict the future is to create it.
Peter Drucker

You can do anything you wish to do, have anything you wish to have, be anything you wish to be.
Robert Collier

Doctors and scientists said that breaking the four-minute mile was impossible, that one would die in the attempt. Thus, when I got up from the track after collapsing at the finish line, I figured I was dead.
Roger Bannister

A leader is one who knows the way, goes the way, and shows the way.
John C. Maxwell
For every good reason there is to lie, there is a better reason to tell the truth. Bo Bennett

In order to succeed, your desire for success should be greater than your fear of failure.
Bill Cosby

Regardless of who you are or what you have been, you can be what you want to be.
W. Clement Stone

The secret of success in life is for a man to be
ready for his opportunity when it comes.
Benjamin Disraeli

You were born to win, but to be a winner, you must plan to win, prepare to win, and expect to win.
Zig Ziglar

Discipline is the bridge between goals and accomplishment.
Jim Rohn

If you will not believe in yourself, then why should anyone else?
Felix Dennis

Action speaks louder than words but not nearly as often.
Mark Twain

Successful people are always looking for opportunities to help others. Unsuccessful people are asking, What's in it for me?
Brian Tracy

Always listen to experts. They'll tell you what can't be done and why. Then do it.
Robert Heinlein

A goal is a dream with a deadline.
Napoleon Hill

Entrepreneurship is neither a science nor an art.
It is a practice.
Peter Drucker

The function of leadership is to produce more
leaders, not more followers.
Ralph Nader

Act enthusiastic and you will be enthusiastic.
Dale Carnegie

"One can't believe impossible things." "I daresay
you haven't had much practice," said the Queen.
"When I was your age, I always did it for half an
hour a day. Why, sometimes I've believed as
many as six impossible things before breakfast."
Lewis Carroll

You take on the responsibility for making your
dream a reality.
Les Brown

You're only here for a short visit. Don't hurry,
don't worry. And be sure to smell the flowers
along the way.
Walter Hagen

The superior man is modest in his speech, but
exceeds in his actions.
Confucius

One doesn't discover new lands without
consenting to lose sight of the shore for a very
long time.
André Gide

Don't just read the easy stuff. You may be
entertained by it, but you will never grow from it.
Jim Rohn

Tell the world what you intend to do, but first
show it.
Napoleon Hill

If you always do what you've always done, you'll
always get what you've always got!
Alan Scott

Vision without action is daydreaming and action without vision is a nightmare. Anon

Success is getting what you want. Happiness is wanting what you get.
Dale Carnegie

Without continual growth and progress, such words as improvement, achievement, and success have no meaning.
Benjamin Franklin

If you want to reach a goal, you must "see the reaching" in your own mind before you actually arrive at your goal.
Zig Ziglar

The few who do are the envy of the many who only watch.
Jim Rohn

An ounce of action is worth a ton of theory.
Ralph Waldo Emerson

There is only one success – to be able to spend your life in your own way.
Christopher Morley

The way to get started is to quit talking and begin doing.
Walt Disney

Try, try, try, and keep on trying is the rule that must be followed to become an expert in anything.
W. Clement Stone

Big pay and little responsibility are circumstances seldom found together.
Napoleon Hill

Every choice you make has an end result.
Zig Ziglar

Every man paddle his own canoe.
Frederick Marryat

You won't get anything unless you have the vision to imagine it.
John Lennon

"Never give in" is a useful catchphrase. But don't take it too literally. We must all surrender at some time. But never give in easily. If you can, attempt one step farther down the road than appears sensible before giving in.
Felix Dennis

Ideas can be life-changing. Sometimes all you need to open the door is just one more good idea.
Jim Rohn

If everything seems under control, you're just not going fast enough.
Mario Andretti

Coming together is a beginning. Keeping together is progress. Working together is success.
Henry Ford

Success is the maximum utilization of the ability that you have.
Zig Ziglar

The road to success and the road to failure are almost exactly the same.
Colin R. Davis

Success is how high you bounce after you hit bottom.
General George Patton

If you are going to ask yourself life-changing questions, be sure to do something with the answers.
Bo Bennett

In the modern world of business, it is useless to be a creative, original thinker unless you can also sell what you create.
David Ogilvy

Positive thinking will let you do everything better than negative thinking will.
Zig Ziglar

In the realm of ideas everything depends on enthusiasm. In the real world all rests on perseverance.
Johann Wolfgang von Goethe

Every morning I get up and look through the Forbes list of the richest people in America. If I'm not there, I go to work.
Robert Orben

I've learned that mistakes can often be as good a teacher as success.
Jack Welch

I can accept failure, everyone fails at something. But I can't accept not trying.
Michael Jordan

Face reality as it is, not as it was or as you wish it to be.
Jack Welch

As a rule, we find what we look for; we achieve what we get ready for.
James Cash Penney

Money won't make you happy... but everybody wants to find out for themselves.
Zig Ziglar

It is always the start that requires the greatest effort.
James Cash Penney

If you are not willing to risk the unusual, you will have to settle for the ordinary.
Jim Rohn

If you don't have a competitive advantage, don't compete.
Jack Welch

Happiness is that state of consciousness which proceeds from the achievement of one's values.
Ayn Rand

How wonderful it is that nobody need wait a single moment to improve the world.
Anne Frank

If you can DREAM it, you can DO it.
Walt Disney

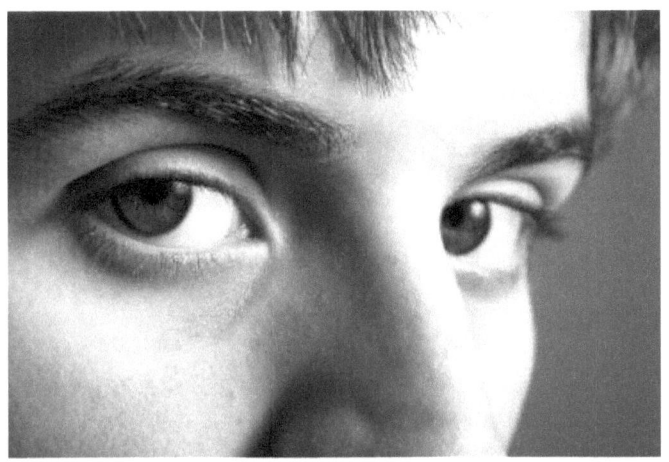

Stubbornness is not persistence. Stubbornness implies you intend to persist despite plentiful evidence that you should not.
Felix Dennis

Buddha left a road map, Jesus left a road map,
Krishna left a road map, Rand McNally left a road
map. But you still have to travel the road
yourself.
Stephen Levine

To change one's life. Start immediately.
Do it flamboyantly. No Exceptions.
William James

If you want to feel rich, just count all of the
things you have that money can't buy.
Anon.

It's kind of fun to do the impossible.
Walt Disney

What lies behind us and what lies before us are
small matters to what lies within us.
Ralph Waldo Emerson

People are like stained-glass windows. They
sparkle and shine when the sun is out, but when
the darkness sets in, their true beauty is revealed
only if there is a light from within.
Elizabeth Kübler-Ross

And the trouble is, if you don't risk anything, you risk even more.
Erica Jong

A dream is just a dream. A goal is a dream with a plan and a deadline.
Harvey Mackay

Failure is not about insecurity. It's about lack of execution.
Jeffrey Gitomer

Better understated than overstated. Let people be surprised that it was more than you promised and easier than you said.
Jim Rohn

Men often become what they believe themselves to be. If I believe I cannot do something, it makes me incapable of doing it. But when I believe I can, then I acquire the ability to do it even if I didn't have it in the beginning.
Gandhi

No person was ever honored for what he received. Honor has been the reward for what he gave.
Calvin Coolidge

Worry is like a rocking chair: it gives you something to do, but it doesn't get you anywhere.
Dorothy Galyean

Destiny is not a matter of chance, it is a matter of choice. It is not a thing to be waited for, it is a thing to be achieved.
Jeremy Kitson

We would worry less about what others think of us if we realized how seldom they do.
Ethel Barrett

The time is always right to do what is right.
Martin Luther King, Jr.

Success breeds success. Attend to your mind's most joyful, effective discovery process. Bolster the self-beliefs that add confidence, lucidity, and tenacity to your efforts. You'll get more out of what you notice, so heed whatever gives you wisdom.
Marsha Sinetar

I couldn't wait for success, so I went ahead without it.
Jonathan Winters

I'd say it's been my biggest problem all my life.
It's money. It takes a lot of money to make these
dreams come true.
Walt Disney

Ability may get you to the top, but it takes
character to keep you there.
John Wooden

Learn to get in touch with the silence within
yourself, and know that everything in this life has
purpose. There are no mistakes, no coincidences.
All events are blessings given to us to learn from.
Elizabeth Kübler-Ross

All the darkness in the world cannot put out the
light of a single candle.
Unknown

Nothing great was ever achieved without
enthusiasm.
Ralph Waldo Emerson
Think big, act small. A successful and naturally
modest entrepreneur is an object of reverence
and respect in the business world.
Felix Dennis

I learned this, at least, by my experiment: that if one advances confidently in the direction of his dreams, and endeavors to live the life which he had imagined, he will meet with a success unexpected in common hours.
Henry David Thoreau

Whatever you can do or dream you can, begin it. Boldness has genius, power, and magic in it. Begin it now.
Goethe

I have often been adrift, but I have always
stayed afloat.
David Berry

Plodding wins the race
Aesop

I think there is something more important than
believing: Action! The world is full of dreamers.
There aren't enough who will move ahead and
take concrete steps to actualize their vision.
W. Clement Stone

When you get into a tight place and everything
goes against you, 'til it seems as though you
could not hang on a minute longer, never give up
then, for it is just the place and time that the tide
will turn.
Harriet Beecher Stowe

Most of the shadows of this life are caused by
standing on one's own sunshine.
Ralph Waldo Emerson

You can't make someone else's choices. You
shouldn't let someone else make yours.
General Colin Powell

Perfection is achieved, not when there is nothing
left to add, but when there is nothing left to take
away.
Antoine de St. Exupery

You will do foolish things, but do them with enthusiasm.
Colette

Begin somewhere; you cannot build a reputation on what you intend to do.
Liz Smith

You may have to fight a battle more than once to win it.
Margaret Thatcher

God gives us talent; work transforms talent into genius.
Anna Pavlova

Getting rich comes from an attitude of mind. It isn't going to happen if things drift on pretty much the way they are right now.
Felix Dennis

Success is never permanent; failure is never fatal. The only thing that really counts is to never, never, never give up.
Sir Winston Churchill

You gain strength, courage and confidence by every experience in which you really stop to look fear in the face... You must do the thing which you think you cannot do.
The future belongs to those who believe in the beauty of their dreams.
Eleanor Roosevelt

I want to do it because I want to do it.
Amelia Earhart

It had long since come to my attention that people of accomplishment rarely sat back and let things happen to them. They went out and happened to things.
Elinor Smith

It doesn't matter what you are thinking or what fear you have, if you just do it. Action is the only thing that matters. I can see that at the end of my life, I'm going to look back and say, "Gosh, I wish I had taken more action."
Diana von Welanetz Wentworth

Your most unhappy customers are your greatest source of learning.
Bill Gates

If you do build a great experience, customers tell each other about that. Word of mouth is very powerful.
Jeff Bezos

Many great ideas go unexecuted, and many great executioners are without ideas. One without the other is worthless.
Tim Blixseth

I've always worked very, very hard, and the harder I worked, the luckier I got.
Alan Bond

Make your product easier to buy than your competition, or you will find your customers buying from them, not you.
Mark Cuban

Doubt, of whatever kind, can be ended by action alone.
Thomas Carlyle

In order to change, we must be sick and tired of being sick and tired.
Anon.

If at first you don't succeed, try, try, try again.
W.E. Hickson

Whenever you see a successful business,
someone once made a courageous decision.
Peter Drucker

You can't expect to hit the jackpot if you don't
put some nickels in the machine.
Flip Wilson

"Mean to" don't pick no cotton.
Anon.

Above all, try something.
Franklin D. Roosevelt.

Do it big, or stay in bed.
Larry Kelly

Let us be brave in the face of adversity.
Seneca

I do not believe a man can ever leave his
business. He ought to think of it by day and
dream of it by night.
Henry Ford

He's no failure. He's not dead yet.
W. L. George.

Continuous effort – not strength or intelligence –
is the key to unlocking our potential
Sir Winston Churchill.

Only those who dare to fail greatly can ever
achieve greatly.
Robert F Kennedy

It is the business of the future to be dangerous.
Alfred North Whitehead

What counts is not necessarily the size of the dog
in the fight, but the size of the fight in the dog.
Dwight. D. Eisenhower.

Anyone can hold the helm when the sea is calm.
Publius Syrus.

Forget mistakes. Forget failure. Forget everything
except what you're going to do now and do it.
Today is your lucky day.
Will Durant

Entrepreneurs average 3.9 failures before final
success. What sets the successful ones apart is
their amazing persistence. There are a lot of
people out there with good and marketable ideas,
but pure entrepreneurial types almost never
accept defeat.
Lisa M Amos

You'll never find a better sparring partner than
adversity.
Walt Schmidt.

We learn courageous action by going forward
whenever fear urges us to go back. A little boy
was asked how he learned to skate. "By getting
up every time I fell down," he answered.
David Seabury

You will perceive just how much money there is
in the world and how pitifully easy it is to obtain
it. Money that already has your name on it.
Felix Dennis

Life affords no higher pleasures than that of
surmounting difficulties.
Samuel Johnson

A problem well stated is a problem half solved.
Charles F Kettering.
We must dare, and dare again, and go on daring.
Georges Jacques Danton

It's just another crisis
Rupert M. Hart

Failure is an event, not a person.
William D Brown

We should not let our fears hold us back from
pursuing our hopes.
John F Kennedy

Change is what people fear most.
Fyodor Dostoyevsky

One ought never to turn one's back on a threatened danger and try to run away from it. If you do that, you will double any danger. But if you meet it promptly and without flinching, you will reduce the danger by half. Never run away from anything. Never!
Sir Winston Churchill

The future is here. It's just not evenly distributed yet.
William Gibson

Of all the sad words of tongue or pen, the saddest are these: It might have been.
John Greenleaf Whittier

There is no data on the future.
Laurel Cutler

Everyone gets their rough day. No one gets a free ride. Today so far, I had a good day. I got a dial tone.
Rodney Dangerfield.

We must dare to have unthinkable thoughts.
James W Fulbright.

I'm in wonderful position: I'm unknown, I'm underrated, and there's nowhere to go but up.
Pierre DuPont IV

It is the greatest shot of adrenaline to be doing what you've wanted to do so badly. You almost feel like you could fly without the plane.
Charles Lindbergh

Morale is the greatest single factor in successful wars.
Dwight D. Eisenhower

I have always been delighted at the prospect of a new day, a fresh try, one more start, worth perhaps a bit of magic waiting somewhere behind the morning.
J. B. Priestley

Bravery is the capacity to perform properly even when scared half to death.
General Omar Bradley

Behold the turtle. He makes progress only when he sticks his neck out.
James Conant

Grant me the courage not to give up even though
I think it is hopeless.
Chester W Nimitz

A leader is a dealer in hope.
Napoleon Bonaparte

Let me tell you the secret that has led me to my
goal. My strength lies solely in my tenacity.
Louis Pasteur

To keep a lamp burning we have to keep putting
oil in it.
Mother Teresa

Failure is something made only by those who fail
to dare, not by those who dare to fail.
Anne Morrow Lindbergh

Entrepreneurship – the most fun you can have
with your clothes on.
Anon.

Never confuse a single defeat with final defeat.
F. Scott Fitzgerald.

Success is going from failure to failure without
loss of enthusiasm.
Sir Winston Churchill

Don't look forward to the day when you stop
suffering. Because when it comes, you'll know
you're dead.
Tennessee Williams

Many a man never fails because he never tries.
Norman MacEwan

Without hope men are only half alive. With hope
they dream and think and work.
Charles Sawyer.

The pessimist sees the difficulty in every
opportunity; the optimist sees the opportunity in
every difficulty.
L.P.Jacks

My center is giving way, my right is in retreat:
situation excellent. I am attacking.
Marshal Foch

What if everything went right?
Zen

You must avoid the trap of going into what you
think will make you money if you have no
empathy or feeling for what you are about to do.
Felix Dennis

Enthusiasm can only be aroused by two things:
first, an ideal which takes the imagination by
storm, and second, a definite intelligible plan for
carrying that ideal into practice.
Arnold Toynbee

Nothing happens unless first a dream
Carl Sandburg

Decision and determination are the engineer and
fireman of our train to opportunity and success.
Burt Lawlor

Trust your own instinct. Your mistakes might as
well be your own, instead of someone else's.
Billy Wilder

Be like a postage stamp – stick to one thing 'til
you get there.
Josh Billings

If you break your neck, if you have nothing to eat, if your house is on fire – then you got a problem. Everything else is inconvenience.
Robert Fulghum

To love what you do and feel that it matters – how could anything else be more fun?
Katherine Graham

Eighty percent of success is showing up.
Woody Allen

The tragedy of life is not that it ends so soon, but that we wait so long to begin it.
Anon.

The wave of the future is coming and there is no fighting it.
Anne Morrow Lindbergh

It is the lone worker who makes the first advance in a subject: the details may be worked out by a team, but the prime idea is due to the enterprise, thought and perception of an individual.
Sir Alexander Fleming
Discoverer of penicillin

Many strokes overthrow the tallest oak.
John Lyly

There is nothing more difficult to take in hand,
more perilous to conduct, or more uncertain in its
success, than to take the lead in the introduction
of a new order of things.
Niccolo Machiavelli

Courage is not the absence of fear but the
mastery of it.
Mark Twain

Men do not fail; they stop trying.
Elihu Root.

In embracing change, entrepreneurs ensure
social and economic stability.
George Gilder.

Too busy with the crowded hour to fear to live or
die.
Ralph Waldo Emerson

Some days you tame the tiger. And some days
the tiger has you for lunch.
Tug McGraw.

Vision is the art of seeing the invisible.
Jonathan Swift

Call the roll in your memory of conspicuously
successful business giants and ...you will be
struck by the fact that almost every one of them
encountered inordinate difficulties sufficient to
crush all but the gamest of spirits. Edison went
hungry many times before he became famous.
B. C. Forbes

To know just what has to be done, then to do it, comprises the whole philosophy of practical life.
Sir William Osler

The key to everything is patience. You get the chicken by hatching the egg – not by smashing it.
Arnold Glasgow

Trouble is only opportunity in work clothes.
Henry J Kaiser

To strive, to seek, to find, and not to yield.
Alfred Lord Tennyson

None of us can be free of conflict and woe. Even the greatest men have had to accept disappointments as their daily bread.
Bernard M Baruch

Hope is the last thing that dies in a man.
Francois de la Rochefoucault

If you do what you've always done, you'll get what you've always gotten.
Anon.

You cannot step twice into the same river.
Heraclitus.

Choosing a goal and sticking to it changes
everything.
Scott Reed

We are all in the gutter, but some of are looking
at the stars.
Oscar Wilde.

True happiness...is not attained through self-
gratification, but through fidelity to a worthy
purpose.
Helen Keller

What is more mortifying than to feel that you
have missed the plum for want of courage to
shake the tree?
Logan Pearsall Smith

Don't wait for your ship to come; swim to it.
Anon.

You cannot banish fear, but you can face it down, stomp on it, crush it, bury it, padlock it into the deepest recesses of your heart and soul and leave it there to rot.
Felix Dennis

Effort only fully releases its reward after a person refuses to quit.
Napoleon Hill

Life has no smooth road for any of us.
W. C. Doane

Destiny is what you are supposed to do in life. Fate is what kicks you in the ass to make you do it.
Henry Miller

Failure is not in losing, but in no longer believing that winning is worthwhile.
Anon.

Far and away the best prize that life offers is the chance to work hard at work worth doing.
Theodore Roosevelt

The best way out of a problem is through it.
Anon.

It's no good running a pig farm badly for thirty years while saying "Really I was meant to be a ballet dancer." By that time, pigs will be your style.
Quentin Crisp

I have no private life. I have a wife who understands. When the phone doesn't ring at home I get depressed. So my wife says "Why not go out and sell something, Lew?" And that always cheers me up.
Lord Lew Grade
Media Magnate

A winner never quits, and a quitter never wins.
Anon.

You cannot fight against the future. Time is on
our side.
William Gladstone

A musician must make magic, an artist must
paint, a poet must write, if he is to be ultimately
at peace with himself. What a man can be, he
must be.
Abraham Maslow

Order and simplification are the first steps toward
the mastery of a subject – the actual enemy is
the unknown.
Thomas Mann

Dare to be naïve.
Buckminster Fuller

But I, being poor, have only my dreams;
I have spread my dreams under your feet; Tread
softly because you tread on my dreams.
William Butler Yeats

All progress is based upon a universal innate desire on the part of every organism to live beyond its income.
Samuel Butler

In a calm sea every man is a pilot.
John Ray

An institution is the lengthened shadow of one man.
Ralph Waldo Emerson

Discovery consists of seeing what everybody has seen and thinking what nobody has thought.
Albert Szent-Gyorgi

The will to do, the soul to dare.
Sir Walter Scott
The Lady of the Lake

He wants to leave a scratch on that wall – Kilroy was here – that somebody a hundred, or a thousand years later will see.
William Faulkner

The cat in gloves catches no mice
Benjamin Franklin

'Twixt the optimist and pessimist
The difference is droll
The optimist sees the doughnut
But the pessimist sees the hole.
McLandburgh Wilson

There is the greatest practical benefit in making a
few failures early in life
Thomas Huxley

I am the master of my fate,
I am the captain of my soul.
William Ernest Henley
Echoes

Each problem has hidden in it an opportunity so
powerful that it literally dwarfs the problem. The
greatest success stories were created by people
who recognized a problem and turned it into an
opportunity.
Joseph Sugarman

I've got a great ambition to die of exhaustion
rather than boredom.
Angus Grossart

Innovations come from creative destruction.
Yoshihisa Tabuchi

To be successful, keep looking tanned, live in an elegant building (even if you're in the cellar), be seen in smart restaurants (even if you nurse one drink) and if you borrow, borrow big.
Aristotle Onassis

The only truth about Luck, good or bad, is that it will change.
Felix Dennis

They can because they think they can.
Virgil

To the timid and hesitating everything is impossible because it seems so.
Sir Walter Scott

A great manager has a knack of making ballplayers think they are better than they think they are. He forces you to have a good opinion of yourself. He lets you know he believes in you. He makes you get more out of yourself. And once you learn how good you really are, you never settle for playing anything less than your very best.
Reggie Jackson

If you've got it, flaunt it. If you do not, pretend.
Wally Phillips

They've got us surrounded again, the poor
bastards.
Gen George Creighton W Abrams

Courage is being scared to death...and saddling
up anyway.
John Wayne

We shall draw from the heart of suffering itself
the means of inspiration and survival.
Sir Winston Churchill

The moment one definitely commits oneself,
Providence moves too. All sorts of things occur to
help, that would never otherwise have occurred.
W. H. Murray

Choices are the hinges of destiny.
Edwin Markham

Nature's mighty law is change.
Robert Burns

You have to have a dream so you wake up in the
morning.
Billy Wilder.

The world stands aside to let anyone pass who
knows where he is going.
David Starr Jordan

Whatever course you have chosen for yourself, it
will not be a chore but an adventure if you bring
to it a sense of the glory of striving, if your sights
are set far above the merely secure and
mediocre.
David Sarnoff

Do what you love and the money will follow.
Marsha Sinetar

Every successful person I have heard of has done
the best he could with the conditions as he found
them, and not waited until next year for better.
E W Howe

It takes twenty years to make an overnight success.
Eddie Cantor

As long as you can start, you are all right. The juice will come.
Ernest Hemingway

Pick battles big enough to matter, small enough to win.
Jonathan Kozol

Life is pretty simple: You do some stuff. Most fails. Some works. You do more of what works. If it works big, others quickly copy it. Then you do something else. The trick is the doing of something else.
Tom Peters

If at first you don't succeed, you're running about average.
M H Alderson

The only history that is worth a tinker's damn is what we make today.
Henry Ford

The most important thing in communication is to hear what isn't being said.
Peter F. Drucker

If what you are doing is not moving you towards your goals, then it's moving you away from your goals.
Brian Tracy

The entrepreneur builds an enterprise; the technician builds a job.
Michael Gerber

As long as you're going to be thinking anyway, think big.
Donald Trump

Don't make friends who are comfortable to be with. Make friends who will force you to lever yourself up.
Thomas J. Watson

All achievements, all earned riches, have their beginning in an idea.
Napoleon Hill

Commuter – one who spends life
In riding to and from his wife;
A man who shaves and takes a train
And then rides back to shave again
E.B White
"Commuter"

We all live in a state of ambitious poverty.
Juvenal

At thirty, a man suspects himself a fool; Knows it
at forty, and reforms his plan; At fifty chides his
infamous delay,
Pushes his prudent purpose to resolve; In all the
magnanimity of thought Resolves, and re-
resolves; then dies the same.
Edward Young

The vitality of thought is an adventure. Ideas
won't keep. Something must be done about
them. When the idea is new, its custodians have
fervor, live for it, and, if need be, die for it.
Alfred North Whitehead

Beware of all enterprises that require new
clothes.
Henry David Thoreau

Ideas don't make you rich. The correct execution
of ideas does.
Felix Dennis

We are the music-makers,
And we are the dreamers of dreams,
Wandering by lone sea breakers,
And sitting by desolate streams;
World-losers, and world-forsakers,
On whom the pale moon gleams;
Yet we are the movers and shakers
Of the World forever, it seems.
Arthur O'Shaughnessy

Nothing is more dangerous than an idea, when
it's the only one we have.
Emile Auguste Chartier

It is better to be making the news than taking it;
to be an actor rather than a critic.
Sir Winston Churchill

He that will not apply new remedies must expect
new evils; for time is the greatest innovator.
Francis Bacon

One of the greatest pains to human nature is the
pain of a new idea.

Walter Bagehot
I seen my opportunities and I took 'em.
George Washington Plunkitt

No bird soars too high, if he soars with his wings.
Wlliam Blake

Many times we will get more ideas and better ideas in two hours of creative loafing than in eight hours at a desk.
Wilfred Peterson

The rewards in business go to the man who does something with an idea.
William Benton

When you are going through Hell, keep going.
Sir Winston Churchill

You are the one who must choose his place.
James Lane Allen

Life shrinks or expands in proportion to one's courage.
Anaïs Nin

After all, tomorrow is another day.
Margaret Mitchell
We are continually faced by great opportunities brilliantly disguised as insoluble problems.
Lee Iacocca

The secret of getting ahead is getting started. The secret of getting started is breaking your complex overwhelming tasks into small manageable tasks, and then starting on the first one.
Mark Twain

I owe my success to having listened respectfully to the very best advice, and then going away and doing the exact opposite.
G K Chesterton

Don't think of it as failure, think of it as time-released success.
Robert Orben

One machine can do the work of fifty ordinary men. No machine can do the work of one extraordinary man.
Elbert Hubbard

Most people can do extraordinary things if they have the confidence or take risks. Yet most people don't. They sit in front of the TV and treat life as if it goes on forever.
Philip Adams

No matter how big or soft or warm your bed is, you still have to get out of it.
Grace Slick

Writers are really people who write books not because they are poor, but because they are dissatisfied with the books which they could buy but do not like.
Walter Benjamin

You should hammer your iron while it is hot.
Publius Syrus

And the trouble is, if you don't risk anything, you risk even more.
Erica Jong

To be successful, the first thing you do is fall in love with your work.
Mary Lauretta

Business is like sex. When it's good, it's very, very good; when it's not so good, it's still good.
George Katona

People have a way of becoming what you encourage them to be – not what you nag them to be.
S. N Parker

If you can meet with Triumph and Disaster
And treat those two imposters the same...
If you can talk with crowds and keep your virtue,
Or walk with Kings – nor lose the common touch...
Yours is the Earth and everything that's in it,
And –which is more – you'll be a man, my son!
Rudyard Kipling

But I would not give in. And that was the secret ingredient. I would not be a wage slave. I would not take "no' for an answer. I would not give in. I was going to be rich. Somehow. Some way. Someday soon. And I would not retreat to the safety of a decent job until I was starved out of house and home. I would not give in.
Felix Dennis

A hero is a man who does what he can.
Romain Rolland

To fight a bull when you are not scared is nothing. And to *not* fight a bull when you are scared is nothing. But to fight a bull when you are scared is something.
Anon.

To establish oneself in the world, one has to do all one can to appear established.
Francois de la Rochefoucault

There are risks and costs to a program of action. But they are far less than the long-range risks and costs of comfortable inaction.
John F Kennedy

When I talked, no one listened to me. But as soon as I acted I became persuasive, and I no longer find anyone incredulous.
Giosue Borsi

The only things you regret are the things you didn't do.
Michael Curtiz

Conditions are never just right. People who delay action until all factors are favorable do nothing.
William Feather

Having a dream isn't stupid. It's not having a
dream that's stupid.
Anon.

Unless you enter the tiger's lair, you cannot take
the cubs.
Japanese Proverb

Success is that old ABC – Ability, Breaks and
Courage.
Charles Luckman

I've been polite and I've always shown up.
Somebody asked me if I had any advice for
young people entering the business. I said
"Yeah, show up."
Tom T Hall

Change and growth take place when a person has
risked himself and dares to become involved with
his own life.
Herbert Otto.

155

Taking a new step...is what people fear most.
Fyodor Dostoyevsky.

Shoot for the moon. Even if you miss it you will
land among the stars.
Les Brown.

We cannot escape fear. We can only transform it
into a companion that accompanies us on all our
exciting adventures.
Susan Jeffers.

The saddest words of all are: "it might have
been."

Everyone has been made for some particular
work, and the desire for that work has been put
in every heart.
Rumi.

The characteristic gift that makes us human is
...the gift of imagination.
Jacob Bronowski

Life is either a daring adventure
or it is nothing.
Helen Keller

Who wants to live forever?

We are what we think. All that we are arises with our thoughts. With our thoughts we make the world.
Buddha

Is not life a thousand times too short for us to bore ourselves?
Friedrich Nietzsche

It is only when we realize that life is taking us nowhere that it begins to have meaning.
P.D. Ouspensky.

Not I - not anyone else, can travel that road for you. You must travel it for yourself.
Walt Whitman.

Each entered the forest at a point he, himself, had chosen, where it was darkest and there was no path.
"The Quest of the Holy Grail."

If a man does not keep pace with his companions perhaps it is because he hears a different drummer. Let him step to the music he hears, however measured or far away.
Henry David Thoreau.

Man is not the creature of circumstances. Circumstances are the creatures of men.
Benjamin Disraeli.

Ask and it shall be given unto you. Seek and ye shall find.
Luke 11:9.

The greatest obstacle to being heroic is the doubt whether one may not be going to prove one's self a fool; the truest heroism is to resist the doubt; and the profoundest wisdom to know when it ought to be resisted, and when to be obeyed.
Nathaniel Hawthorne.

Life's most urgent question is, what are you doing for others?
Martin Luther King.

A good novel reads as an interesting plot; so does a good life.
Laurence G. Boldt
"Zen and the art of making a living."

Without vision, the people perish.
Proverbs 29:18

Every great movement must experience three stages: ridicule, discussion, adoption.
John Stuart Mill

The formulation of a problem is far more essential than its solution.
Albert Einstein

What we do is nothing but a drop in the ocean, but if we didn't do it, the ocean would be one drop less.
Mother Teresa of Calcutta.

There is one thing stronger than all the armies in the world, and that is an idea whose time has come.
Voltaire.

No one knows what he can do until he tries.
Publius Syrus

The idea that is not dangerous is unworthy of
being called an idea at all.
Elbert Hubbard.

A man's dreams are an index to his greatness.
Zadok Rabinowitz

For the secret of man's being is not only to live,
but to have something to live for.
Fyodor Dostoyevsky.

Thus to be independent of public opinion is the first formal condition of achieving anything great.
G.W.F Hegel.

Work to become, not to acquire.
Elbert Hubbard.

Few men ever drop dead from overwork, but many quietly curl up and die because of under-satisfaction.
Sidney J. Harris.

It is the chiefest point of happiness that a man is willing to be what he is.
Erasmus.

I will act as if what I do makes a difference.
William James.

The first venture which an entrepreneur undertakes is almost certainly motivated by the very strong ambition of the individual to become independent and recognized by those around him as a success than by any more rational considerations.
David Robinson,
"The Naked Entrepreneur."

Wherefore by their fruits ye shall know them.
Matthew 7:20.

Your work is to discover your work and then with all your heart to give yourself to it.
Buddha.

It's not enough to say "I'm earning enough to live and support my family. I do my work well. I'm a good father. I'm a good churchgoer." That's all very well BUT YOU MUST DO SOMETHING MORE.
Albert Schweitzer.

Live as you will have wished to have lived when you are dying.
Christian Furchtegott Gellert.

In the long run you hit only what you aim at. Therefore, though you should fail immediately, you had better aim at something high.
Henry David Thoreau.

One person with a belief is a social power equal to ninety-nine who have only an interest.
John Stuart Mill.

Every man has his own vocation, talent is the call.
Ralph Waldo Emerson.

It is your work in life that is the ultimate seduction.
Pablo Picasso

If you only care enough for a result, you will almost certainly attain it.
William James

The focused mind can pierce through stone.
Japanese saying.

Do not turn back when you are just at the goal.
Publius Syrus.

There are costs and risks to a program of action, but they are far less than the long range risks and costs of comfortable inaction.
John F. Kennedy.

The trouble with the rat race
is that even if you win
you're still a rat
Lily Tomlin.

I have learned this at least by my experiment:
that if one advances confidently in the direction
of his dreams, and endeavors to live the life
which he has imagined, he will meet with a
success unexpected in common hours.
Henry David Thoreau.

Our aspirations are our possibilities.
Robert Browning.

Find your own set of values. Feel needed. Feel
useful. Feel good. What else in life is there?
Erich Segal.

Always bear in mind that your own resolution to
succeed is more important than any other one
thing.
Abraham Lincoln.

He conquers who endures.
Perseus.

There is no great thought that has become an
impelling history which has not been espoused at
its origin by men willing to put all their physical
and spiritual powers entirely at its service.
Louis Ginsberg.

You are what you do.
Anon.

Every individual has a place to fill in the world
and is important in some respect, whether he
chooses to be so or not.
Nathaniel Hawthorne.

Bravery never goes out of style.
William Thackeray

Many people abandon the ship of their dreams as
soon as they run into the first strong wind.
Laurence G. Boldt.
"Zen and the art of making a living."

Go to the battlefield firmly confident of victory
and you come home with no wound whatsoever.
Kenshin Uesugi,
Samurai general.

Whether you think you can or you can't - you are
right.
Henry Ford.

Approach the moment with the idea that you're
in the fight to the finish.
Mataemon Iso.

Take time to deliberate; but when the time for action arrives, stop thinking and go in.
Andrew Jackson.

The empires of the future are empires of the mind.
Winston Churchill.

A wise man will make more opportunities than he finds.
Francis Bacon.

The entrepreneur essentially is a visualizer and an actualizer. He can visualize something, and when he visualizes it he sees exactly how to make it happen.
Robert Schwartz.

Our greatest glory is not in never falling, but in rising every time we fall.
Confucius.

Winners never quit and quitters never win.

Deliver steak, not just the sizzle.
Michael Maccoby,
"The Leader."

Every man-made thing, however small, started in someone's imagination.

The individual's inability to submit to authority and accept organizational rules...drive him or her to become an entrepreneur.
Manfred Kets De Vries.

A leader must outbid his rivals in self-confidence.
Charles de Gaulle.

I didn't have the slightest idea of how I was going to finance it, but I was sure I'd find a way.
James Goldsmith.

It is necessary to be slightly under-employed if you are going to do something significant.
Watson,
"Double Helix."

Fly with the eagles.

Everyone who can face up to decision-making can learn to be an entrepreneur and to behave entrepreneurially.
Peter Drucker.

I created it that way because I decide what I
want to do, where I want to do it, when I want to
do it, and how it ought to be done. I like that.
Architect/ Developer.

Whatever you do may seem insignificant, but it is
very important that you do it.
Mahatma Gandhi.

At the heart of every entrepreneur
is an Indiana Jones.

He wants his talents and work to be recognized.
Roger Shoshana.

The night is darkest just before dawn.....

I lose my confidence sometimes and that's where
the courage comes in.
Fuqua.

It's not what you get that makes you successful,
it is what you are continuing to do with what
you've got.
Denis Waitley.

We do it, not because it is easy, but because it is hard.
John F. Kennedy
[of the Moon landing]

Actions speak louder than words.
Aesop.

Talk is cheap.

Maintain a restless interest in the incongruous.

To be able to say that you have changed the course of economic development through the introduction of a new material or product is to recognize a special form of power.
David Robinson,
"The Naked Entrepreneur."

Things may come to those who wait, but only the things left by those who hustle.
Abraham Lincoln.

In the sixties, entrepreneurship had come into vogue because of the neat way it reconciled the rebelliousness of the counterculture with the eternal verities of the American Dream.
Frank Rose,
Author of "West of Eden" (history of Apple Computer).

If you're going to drown, don't do it in shallow water.
Bulgarian proverb

What is it that you get excited about? When does the juice really begin to run? That is what has a lot of meaning for you, and that is aligned with your purpose. You must be true to that.
Michael Ray & Rochelle Myers,
Authors of "Creativity in Business"

I call intuition cosmic feeling. You feel a nibble, then you've got to hook the fish.
Buckminster Fuller.

"Do you want to change the world, or sell sugared water?"
Steve Jobs to John Sculley,
persuading him to leave Pepsi to become CEO of Apple Computer.

Everyone must row with the oars he has.
English proverb.

Quiet calm deliberation untangles every knot.
Harold Macmillan,
former British Prime Minister.

Any business is really an "idea machine".
Edward de Bono.

Don't fall in love with an invention or an idea. Ideas are expendable and there's always a new and better one.
Denis Waitley.

The blunt truth is that unless you learn to do at least one thing very well, perhaps a bit better than other people who have the same dreams, there is little chance of attaining lofty goals.

"Son, if they don't like you, they've got bad taste."
Bob Hoskins.

It is essential that your family, friends and business associates pull you toward and not away from your business goals.
Warren Avis.

Never give up on your dreams.

It is our duty as men and women to proceed as though the limits of our abilities do not exist.
Pierre Teilhard de Chardin

Leaders perform many functions, the most important being to articulate to their followers a vision of the future of whatever task they try to accomplish and the means to get there.
Manfred Kets de Vries.

Life is what you make it.

You should look for the spark of originality that makes [you] different from other people, and develop that for all it's worth.
Dale Carnegie.

"You and I will make the impossible happen."
Jay A. Conger,
Author of "The Charismatic Leader"

I never perfected an invention that I did not think about in terms of the service it might give others.
Thomas Alva Edison.

The secret sorrow of his life was that he did not head up a business of his own.
Ayn Rand,
Author of "The Fountainhead"

Think for yourself. What everyone else is doing may not be the right thing.
Aesop.

The heart of the entrepreneur's task is the discovery of something customers will want.
Karl Vesper.

The sensation of being trapped is the ultimate indignity.

There is more than a little Walter Mitty in all of us - we all dream of inventing something.

We are all creative. We all have ideas. All we require is the confidence to prove them.
Roger Shoshana.

The charismatic leader has a sensitivity to constituent's needs... and an unusual ability to see the deficiencies of the existing situation and untapped opportunities.
"The Charismatic Leader",
Jay A. Conger.

The man who wins may have been counted out
several times, but he didn't hear the referee.
H. E. Jansen.

If data is available, it's too late.
Charles Banfe, Author of "Entrepreneur: From
Zero to Hero"

The gift of the innovator is his ability to keep his
attention on what most of us avoid.
Laurence G. Boldt.
"Zen and the art of making a living."

I have a dream.
Martin Luther King.

You can't just sit under the apple tree and let
ideas keep falling on your head.
You've got to shake that apple tree to make
things happen.

Creativity always begins with a question.
The quality of your creativity is determined by
the quality of your questions.
Michael Ray & Rochelle Myers.
"Creativity in Business"

Action makes more fortunes than caution.
Vauvenargues.

Morse made his fortune because his invention
[the telegraph] coincided with the needs of the
nation.

[Creativity] is going to be critical for business. All
the rest is housekeeping.
Edward de Bono
"Sur/Petition."

Today is the best day of my life.
Denis Waitley.

One of the most common mistakes people make
in their careers is that they 'check out too soon."

If you employ people with small thinking and
small ideas, you become a company of dwarves.
David Ogilvy.

They all viewed me, not without reason, as a
loose cannon.
James Goldsmith,
"Billionaire."

Money is no good if you have to work so hard for
it that you don't have time to enjoy it.
Warren Avis.

Experience is the name everyone gives to his
mistakes.
Oscar Wilde,
"Lady Windermere's Fan"

They will rise to the top in spite of all dangers;
they will get the applause; they will find a way to
master their fears.
Manfred Kets de Vries.

Sell the dream.
H. Skip Weitzen.
"Hypergrowth"

Would you rise in the world? You must work while
others amuse themselves.
Churchill
"Savrola"

Dare to be great.
Victor Kiam
Remington

A troubled man visited his rabbi: "I'm a failure. I
do not succeed in what I am doing more than
half the time."
Yet Ty Cobb, greatest baseball slugger of all
time, had a lifetime average of only 0.367 - one
hit out of every three times at bat.
Robert Fulghum.

They have an overriding concern to be heard and recognized, to be seen as heroes. Some entrepreneurs need to show others that they amount to something, that they cannot be ignored.
Manfred Kets De Vries.

The ability to communicate and persuade is an important feature of charismatic leaders.
Jay A. Conger.
Author of "The Charismatic Leader"

Alas, the fearful unbelief in yourself!
Thomas Carlyle.

Think of failure as a resting place, and you're in the proper frame of mind to start a business.
J. Mancuso,
"Fun & Guts: the entrepreneur's philosophy."

It must be something that the community does not know it needs but will want when it hears about it;
Or it must fulfill a known and still unsatisfied need;
Or it must improve upon existing goods and services in a market that believes itself to be well-served.
Karl Vesper.

"What's your track record?"
Your track record is your credit card.
Richard Wrigley, Entrepreneur,
"Whicker's World"

Success is the progressive realization of a worthy
ideal.
Earl Nightingale.

Entrepreneurs in pursuit of their goal are
awesome people. Their adherence to their
mission gives them immeasurable strength.
Roger Shoshana.

All you have to do is offer a product or service
that people need and are willing to buy.
Victor Kiam.
Remington.

A man is as tall as his dreams.

Many people have good business ideas, spot the
opportunities, see the exploitation potential, but
do nothing about it.
David Robinson,
"The Naked Entrepreneur."

The best of all leaders is the one who helps
people so that, emotionally, they don't need
him....when he is finished with his work, the
people say, "it happened naturally."
Lao Tzu.

Imagination is the key.
Charles Banfe,
Author of "Entrepreneur: From Zero to Hero."

To know and not to do is not yet to know.
Zen.

Anything worth doing well is worth doing to
excess.
Edwin Land,
founder of Polaroid Corporation.

Probably 99% of all human ability is wasted.

Why do you have to be so different?
His mother to Bill Lear,
(of "Learjet" fame).

I have found my hero and he is me.

Be what you is, not what you ain't.
'Cause if you ain't what you is, you is what you
ain't.
Luther D. Price.

I asked a very successful friend at our twenty-
fifth alumni reunion of the Harvard Business
School for his measure of success. He said, 'I
learned to smell the roses.'
Robert Medearis,
former Chairman, Silicon Valley Bank.

Now is the best time to be alive.
Denis Waitley.

Entrepreneurs will have to learn to practice
systematic innovation.
Peter Drucker.

The most important characteristic ...is the ability
to recognize and throw away bad ideas.
Otherwise, you will waste a tremendous amount
of time following up bad ideas.
Linus Pauling.

New products and services can arise from any
source:
• from spotting a need not yet filled and turning
it into something real,
• from picking up a technical advance with
limited application and applying it to a new
product,
• from transferring an idea from one market to
another, or
• from radically transforming an existing
product.
Design Council.

Every time, an entrepreneur begins to soar on
the wings of a new idea...Unless I know I'm
going to get a thrill out of a business concept, I
know I should stay away from it.
Warren Avis.

I've been rich and I've been poor. Believe me,
rich is better.
Sophie Tucker.

Imitate the sundial's ways,
Count only the pleasant days.

If you can dream and not make dreams your
master...
Rudyard Kipling
"If.."

I am immortal 'til my work is done.
General Gordon.

It has always been a matter of debate as to
whether great men make history or the sweep of
historical events makes great men.

A mighty teacher is adversity.
"Sweat Morden"

If God be for us, who can be against us?
Romans 8:31.

A self-sufficient ego.
Nothing else matters.
Ayn Rand.
"Fountainhead."

Don't try to be something you are not.
Aesop.

To go from the idea to the prototype is in some
cases a major hurdle. But to go from the
prototype to the product - that is the mountain.
Karl Vesper.

Marconi, by his own admission, experimented
with devices invented by other men and applied
certain improvements to these.
Design Council exhibit.

G.O.Y.A.
Get Off Your Ass.

Liberation finally amounts to being free from things we don't like in order to be enslaved by things we approve of.
Robert Fulghum.

If you can do it, you should do it.
Jane Walmsley.

The chief ingredients of success are imagination, plus ambition, and the will to work.
Thomas Alva Edison.

The successful utilize the raw emotion of the feeling that they have been done down in some way.
Roger Shoshana.

If we have a talent, and cannot use it, we have failed.
If we have a talent, and learn somehow to use all of it, we have gloriously succeeded, and won a satisfaction and a triumph few individuals ever know.
Tom Wolfe.

The entrepreneur is the guy who is personally guaranteeing $5 million but has about $5 in his pocket.
Charles Banfe,
Author, "Entrepreneur: From Zero to Hero."

I think recognition is probably the least
acknowledged and one of the most powerful
propulsions for those who succeed.
Malcolm Forbes.

It was wonderful to have such a positive
indication that I had got it right, that I was right
to trust my gut instinct, that we were providing
products that people wanted and charging a price
they were willing to pay and still enable us to
make profit. To me that was bliss.
Anita Roddick,
founder of "The Body Shop."

Very interesting, Whittle, my boy, but it will
never work.
Professor of Aeronautical Engineering at
Cambridge University to Frank Whittle, inventor
of the jet engine.

Awareness of anomaly [is critical]
Thomas Kuhn.

One intense hour will do more than dreary years.
Henry Ward Beecher.

Happy is the man who has found his right place
and task.

The ultimate entrepreneurial strategic weapon is flexibility.
Peters and Waterman.

George had a career, but Cathy had a CAUSE.
Erich Segal,
"The Class."

You have no responsibility to live up to what other people think you ought to accomplish.
Richard Feynman.

The worst bankrupt in the world is the person who has lost his enthusiasm.
H. W. Arnold.

How will this further your Definite Chief Aim in life?
"Sweat Morden."

Do I need anyone's approval?
Ayn Rand.
"Fountainhead."

What do you care what others think?
Richard Feynman.

It is often easier to have ideas than to carry them out.
Aesop.

$V = P \times S \times E$
The value of a business concept is determined by the size of the problem, the elegance of the solution and the entrepreneurial team.
A. David Silver

If you think money can't buy you happiness, you've been shopping in the wrong places.
Jane Walmsley.

American history is the art of the possible in the land of opportunity.

Success is achieved by those who try.
W. Clement Stone.

Our staff had the good looks and charisma which the adventure business acquires and creates.
Roger Shoshana.

In great attempts, it is glorious even to fail.
Proverb.

A word grows to a thought,
A thought to an idea,
An idea to an act.
Beryl Markham,
"West with the Night"

I have seen the future...
And it's still in the future.

You must have the free time to allow valuable
ideas to bubble up.
Charles Banfe,
Author of "Entrepreneur: From Zero to Hero."

A man is what he thinks about all day long.
Ralph Waldo Emerson.

He was a leader of leaders.
Ovid.

In his desire to bring change, the charismatic
often alienates the forces that represent the
status quo. These vested interests may unify and
later mobilize against the leader.
Jay A. Conger,
Author of "The Charismatic Leader"

If you can't identify who the customer is, how can you invent a product that will satisfy their needs?
William Davidow.

I have succeeded before and I will succeed today.
Richard Conner,
"Getting new clients."

Ask "innocent" questions.
Gary Hamel & C. K. Prahalad.

[About Henry Kaiser and the construction of Liberty ships during World War II]:
Only 194 days after he had entered the shipbuilding business, Kaiser was turning out 10,500 ton Liberties in only 46 days - a quarter of the time it took to build a ship by conventional methods. People become constrained by their egos. They forget the truth. They forget that they were born in the city of the body to do some great work.
Michael Ray & Rochelle Myers,
"Creativity in Business."

If I could live my life again...!

Be special [my mother said]. Be anything but mediocre.
Anita Roddick
founder of "The Body Shop."

We are not here to sell a parcel of boilers and vats, but the potentiality of growing rich beyond the dreams of avarice.
Samuel Johnson.

If you think you can, you can.
None but he knows what he is, which he can do, nor does he know until he has tried.
Ralph Waldo Emerson.

Get all the education you can.
Lee Iacocca.

Procrastination is the thief of time.

Most [people] will continue to
wonder...dream...and wish.
W. Clement Stone.

Having eyes do you not see, and
Having ears do you not hear?
Jesus.

Entrepreneurs: their willingness to seize the
initiative sets them apart from their
contemporaries. They don't sit on their haunches,
waiting for something to happen. They make
things happen.
Victor Kiam,
Remington.

Leaders have ideas.
Max De Pree,
"Leadership is an Art."

When somebody tells you that something can't be done, all it really means is that it hasn't been done before.
Charles Banfe,
Author of "Entrepreneur: From Zero to Hero."

The entrepreneur: seldom lovable but always exciting to work with.
David Robinson,
Author of "The Naked Entrepreneur".

Success is a journey not a destination.
Ben Sweetland.

Mediocrity is fine - so long as it's on schedule!
Frank Rose,
"West of Eden."

[Airplanes:] It was the first time something in his life had captured his imagination so completely.
(of Bill Lear, of Learjet fame).
"Stormy Genius" by Richard Raske.

When a device is properly augmented so that it can be easily sold and used by a customer it becomes a product.
William Davidow.

Ask the right basic questions.

Because he does not compete he does not meet competition.
You owe it to yourself.

Ideally late starters have a larger base of experience upon which to build a career, because they have learned a little bit about a lot...

The good old days are here and now.

After I have launched a company, I tend to turn to new opportunities...I have started to concentrate more on lining up top managers ...to take over when I decide to go onto new ventures. My guess is that I could be worth a hundred times more money if I had just learned to do this years ago.
Warren Avis.

Bankers are just like everyone else, only richer.
Ogden Nash,
From "I'm a stranger here myself."

[Charismatic people are] all people with inspirational gifts, individuals who could impose themselves on their environment, and who stand out because of their extraordinary insight, courage, energy and decisiveness.
Manfred Kets De Vries.

Someday I'll...

There is nothing more difficult...than to take the lead in the introduction of a new order of things. Because the innovator has for enemies all those who have done well under the old conditions...
Niccolo Machiavelli.

Fame is the spur.
Winston Churchill.

We cannot direct the wind, but we can adjust the
sails.
Dolly Parton

You haven't lost. You just haven't won yet.

The battlefield ages men quickly, and that is
where I come from.
Napoleon.

If you want to find a way up the mountain, seek
someone who has taken that road.
Li Po
Chinese poet.

The test of our progress is not whether we add
more to the abundance of those who have much;
it is whether we provide enough for those who
have too little.
Franklin D. Roosevelt.

Knockout success can be achieved by a well-
developed concept, which is the left hook, and
good execution, which is the right cross.
Charles Banfe,
Author, "Entrepreneur: From Zero to Hero."

Artists of every kind discover early that good
things move in when fear moves out.
Michael Ray & Rochelle Myers,
"Creativity in Business."

The crowd is always wrong.

Remember how successfully you helped your clients. You wouldn't deny these types of benefits to these just because they're not fully acquainted with you yet?
Richard Conner,
"Getting new clients."

Steve Jobs made Apple itself different. He was the hero saving the world from domination by the men in gray suits.
William Davidow.

Emulate Alexander the Great's attitude to the Gordian Knot.

It's no use having a marvelous idea and risking all your resources on it only to fail miserably in its practical delivery. [The entrepreneur must be innovator, risk-taker and manager].
David Robinson,
"The Naked Entrepreneur."

The more faithfully you listen to the voice within you, the better you will hear what is sounding outside.
Dag Hammerskjold,

former Secretary General, United Nations.

I'm no genius. I'm smart in spots. I stay around those spots.
Thomas Watson, Jr.,
IBM.

Faith in one's destiny is among the most valuable of the gifts which the gods could bestow upon a man.
Arthur C. Clarke.

One man with a vision - or two brothers- could change the world.
William Davidow.

Charisma - one of the most powerful predictors of success.
"Frontiers of Leadership",
ed. Michael Synett & Clare Hogg.

Apple is one of the greatest business stories of the century.
Newsweek.

Their swashbuckling charm and risk-taking
heroism were appealing.
Jay A. Conger,
"The Charismatic Leader"

Think about your ultimate goal. Make that image
strong. A grin comes from the glow of satisfaction
you earn with success.
Victor Kiam.

Inadequate problem formulation is a major cause
of new business failures.
A. David Silver.

"My mother says I was lucky. No: millions of
people in Kansas City could have taken
advantage of the opportunity, but I recognized it
and they didn't. It's not just luck."
Karl Vesper.

Freedom is more important than comfort.
Aesop.
The degree of a man's independence, initiative
and personal love for his work determines his
talent as a worker and his worth as a man.
Ayn Rand.

Chance favors the prepared mind.
Louis Pasteur.

Believe in what you are doing and you too will
see the great effect of your belief upon those
whom you may request to help you.
"Sweat Morden."

A visionary entrepreneur is spurred on by a
general dissatisfaction with the way things are in
the world.
David Robinson,
"The Naked Entrepreneur."

Raise your sights!
Blaze new trails!
Hit the ball out of the park!
Compete with the immortals!
David Ogilvy.

Be happy while you're living, for you're a long
time dead.
Scottish parable.

Rules are for rulers. Whatever works is for
entrepreneurs.
Bill Foster, Founder
Stratus Computer.

The leader must have infectious optimism, and the determination to persevere in the face of difficulties. He must also radiate confidence, even when he himself is not certain of the outcome.
Field Marshal Montgomery.

Set an overall goal, then set a number of smaller intermediate objectives that are accomplished first.

How do you recognize the right business opportunity for you? In my mind the question falls in the same category as "how do you know when you're going to marry?', or "how do you know when you are in love?" Well - you know!
Robert A. Swanson.
founder of Genentech.

Almost always [the hoped-for market] emerges more slowly than anticipated.
Gary Hamel & C.K. Prahalad.

You might be the Fred Astaire of the business world, but in order to prove it to others you need a stage on which to dance. Don't worry about salary so long as it's enough to pay the bills. Put your pride in your back pocket and opt for opportunity.
Victor Kiam,
Remington.

See yourself rendering the service. Delivering the merchandise. See yourself receiving the payment.
Sweat Morden.

Man's mind, once stretched by a new idea, never regains its original dimensions.
Oliver Wendell Holmes.

Failures are divided into 2 classes: those who thought and never did, and those who did and never thought.
John Charles Salach

Enter muddied, uncertain markets. If there is clarity, someone else is there.
Charles Banfe,
Author of "Entrepreneur: From Zero to Hero."

Most of us accept career conformity as an
unavoidable trade-off of professionalism.
Amy Saltzmann,
Author of "Downshifting"'

It is our duty as men and women to proceed as
though the limits of our abilities do not exist.
Pierre Teilhard de Chardin.

What is robbing a bank compared to founding a
bank?
Bertold Brecht

When you reach an obstacle, turn it into an
opportunity. You have the choice. You can
overcome and be a winner, or you can allow it to
overcome you and be a loser. The choice is yours
and yours alone. Refuse to throw in the towel. Go
that extra mile that failures refuse to travel. It is
far better to be exhausted from success than to
be rested from failure.
Mary Kay Ash, founder of Mary Kay Cosmetics

The critical ingredient is getting off your butt and doing something. It's as simple as that. A lot of people have ideas, but there are few who decide to do something about them now. Not tomorrow. Not next week. But today. The true entrepreneur is a doer, not a dreamer.
Nolan Bushnell, founder of Atari and Chuck E. Cheese's

Business opportunities are like buses, there's always another one coming.
Richard Branson, founder of Virgin Enterprises

Innovation is the specific tool of entrepreneurs, the means by which they exploit change as an opportunity for a different business or a different service. It is capable of being presented as a discipline, capable of being learned, capable of being practiced.
Entrepreneurs need to search purposefully for the sources of innovation, the changes and their symptoms that indicate opportunities for successful innovation. And they need to know and to apply the principles of successful innovation.
Peter F. Drucker

I never perfected an invention that I did not think about in terms of the service it might give others... I find out what the world needs, then I proceed to invent.
Thomas Edison

The important thing is not being afraid to take a chance. Remember, the greatest failure is to not try. Once you find something you love to do, be the best at doing it.
Debbi Fields, founder of Mrs. Fields Cookies

We were young, but we had good advice and good ideas and lots of enthusiasm.
Bill Gates

Entrepreneurs are risk takers, willing to roll the dice with their money or reputation on the line in support of an idea or enterprise. They willingly assume responsibility for the success or failure of a venture and are answerable for all its facets.
Victor Kiam, Remington

If it really was a no-brainer to make it on your own in business there'd be millions of no-brained, hare-brained, and otherwise dubiously-brained individuals quitting their day jobs and hanging out their own shingles. Nobody would be left to round out the workforce and execute the business plan.
Bill Rancic, winner on Donald Trump's The Apprentice

Nobody talks about entrepreneurship as survival, but that's exactly what it is and what nurtures creative thinking. Running that first shop taught me business is not financial science; it's about trading: buying and selling.
Anita Roddick,
founder of "The Body Shop"

I have always found that my view of success has been iconoclastic: success to me is not about money or status or fame, its about finding a livelihood that brings me joy and self-sufficiency and a sense of contributing to the world.
Anita Roddick

Experience taught me a few things. One is to listen to your gut, no matter how good something sounds on paper. The second is that you're generally better off sticking with what you know. And the third is that sometimes your best investments are the ones you don't make.
Donald Trump

I had to make my own living and my own opportunity! But I made it! Don't sit down and wait for the opportunities to come. Get up and make them!
Ms C.J. Walker, America's first black female millionaire

The longer you're not taking action the more money you're losing.
Carrie Wilkerson

Most great people have attained their greatest success just one step beyond their greatest failure.
Napoleon Hill

Go Big, or Go Home.
Eliza Dushku

Opportunity is missed by most people because it is dressed in overalls and looks like work.
Thomas Edison

Have the end in mind and every day make sure you're working towards it.
Ryan Allis

He who begins many things, finishes but few.
German Proverb

The best use of life is to spend it for something that outlasts it.
William James

Entrepreneurship is living a few years of your life like most people won't so you can spend the rest of your life like most people can't.

To never forget that the most important thing in life is the quality of life we lead – Tony Hsieh

It's better to own the racecourse then the race horse.

It's easier to ask forgiveness than it is to get permission.
Grace Hopper

Keep away from people who try to belittle your ambitions. Small people always do that, but the really great make you feel that you, too, can become great. Mark Twain

There is only one success—to be able to spend your life in your own way. Christopher Morley

You don't buy a nice car and get rich; you get rich and buy a nice car.

To win without risk is to triumph without glory.
Corneille

Fall seven times, stand up eight.
Japanese Proverb

One day your life will flash before your eyes. Make sure it is worth watching.
Mooie

Whatever the mind can conceive and believe, the mind can achieve.
Napoleon Hill

I have not failed. I've just found 10,000 ways that won't work.
Thomas Alva Edison

If you ain't making waves, you ain't kickin' hard enough.

What is not started will never get finished.
Wolfgang von Goethe.

Do not wait to strike until the iron is hot; but make it hot by striking.
William B. Sprague

When you cease to dream you cease to live.
Malcolm Forbes

At the point in life where your talents meet the needs of the world is where God wants you to be.
Albert Schweitzer

You either have to be first, best, or different.
Loretta Lynn

I skate to where the puck is going to be, not where it has been.
Wayne Gretzky

A leader is powerful to the degree he empowers other people.
I Ching

It is not the strongest of the species that survive, nor the most intelligent, but the one most responsive to change.
Charles Darwin

To be happy you need: Something to do, someone to love, and something to look forward to.

The road to success is always under construction.
Lily Tomlin

Never ignore a gut feeling, but never believe it is enough.
Bob Heller.

He wanted fame and fortune, not a steady boring job, but he couldn't see a way to get them.
Richard Raske,
Author of biography of Bill Lear

Our success has really been based on partnerships from the very beginning.
Bill Gates

An entrepreneur tends to bite off a little more than he can chew hoping he'll quickly learn how to chew it.
Roy Ash, cofounder of Litton Industries

It's how many things you do right, not how many things you do wrong, that counts.
Sandra Kurtzig

You miss 100% of the shots you never take.
Wayne Gretzky

Do not let what you cannot do interfere with what you can do.
John Wooden

The cover-your-butt mentality of the workplace will get you only so far. The follow-your-gut mentality of the entrepreneur has the potential to take you anywhere you want to go or run you right out of business but it's a whole lot more fun, don't you think?
Bill Rancic

Twenty years from now you will be more disappointed by the things that you didn't do than by the ones you did.
Mark Twain

If you don't paddle your own canoe, you don't move.
Katharine Hepburn

Nothing will work unless you do.
Maya Angelou

Great faith. Great doubt. Great effort.
The Little Zen Companion

The only place where success comes before work
is in a dictionary.
Vidal Sassoon

Out of clutter, find simplicity. From discord, find
harmony. In the middle of difficulty lies
opportunity.
Albert Einstein's three rules of work

A really important part of competition is coming
back, trying to do it better the second time than
you did the first.
Brian Boitano

You may be disappointed if you fail, but you are
doomed if you don't try.
Beverly Sills

The way I see it, if you want the rainbow, you
gotta put up with the rain.
Dolly Parton

Adversity causes some men to break, and others to break records.

What gets us into trouble is not what we don't know. It's what we know for sure that just ain't so.
Yogi Berra

When you get to a fork in the road, take it.
Yogi Berra

If you don't know where you're going, you will wind up somewhere else.

You gain strength, courage and confidence by every experience in which you really stop to look fear in the face ... You must do the thing you think you cannot do.
Eleanor Roosevelt

If you're in a hole, you ought to stop digging.

Every exit is an entry somewhere else. Tom Stoppard

Living well is the best revenge.
George Herbert

When bad things have happened to you, just
remember GOIMO — Get Over It and Move On.
Martha Kanter

Entrepreneurship is living a few years of your life
like most people won't, so that you can spend the
rest of your life like most people can't.

The future belongs to those who believe in the
beauty of their dreams.
Eleanor Roosevelt

The best reason to start an organization is to
make meaning, to create a product or service to
make the world a better place.
Guy Kawasaki

Every worthwhile accomplishment, big or little,
has its stages of drudgery and triumph; a
beginning, a struggle and a victory.
Mahatma Gandhi.

Failure defeats losers, failure inspires winners.
Robert T. Kiyosaki

Entrepreneurs average 3.6 failures before final success. What sets the successful ones apart is their amazing persistence.
Lisa M. Amos

Once you say you're going to settle for second, that's what happens to you in life.
John F. Kennedy

In preparing for battle I have always found that plans are useless, but planning is indispensable.
Dwight D. Eisenhower

The greatest reward in becoming a millionaire is not the amount of money that you earn. It is the kind of person that you have to become to become a millionaire in the first place.
Jim Rohn

Some people dream of great accomplishments, while others stay awake and do them.

The entrepreneur in us sees opportunities everywhere we look, but many people see only problems everywhere they look. The entrepreneur in us is more concerned with discriminating between opportunities than he or she is with failing to see the opportunities.
Michael Gerber

I will tell you how to become rich. Close the doors. Be fearful when others are greedy. Be greedy when others are fearful.
Warren Buffett

Great Books to Read

"The Entrepreneurial Spirit", A. David Silver.

"Zen and the Art of Making a Living : A Practical Guide to Creative Career Design", Laurence G. Boldt

"Begin it now", Susan Hayward.

"The Artist's Way: A Spiritual Path to Higher Creativity", Julia Cameron.

"From Zero to Hero," Charles Banfe

"The Naked Entrepreneur", David Robinson

"The Leader: A New Face for American Management," Michael Maccoby

"The Charismatic Leader : Behind the Mystique of Exceptional Leadership",Jay Alden Conger.

"Living Juicy : Daily Morsels for Your Creative Soul", Sark.

"Feel the Fear and Do It Anyway", Susan Jeffers

"The Psychology of Winning," Denis Waitley

"Seeds of Greatness," Denis Waitley

"On Becoming a Leader," Warren Bennis

"Creativity in Business," Michael Ray & Rochelle Myers.

"Think and Grow Rich," Napoleon Hill.

"New Venture Strategies," Karl Vesper.

"Corporate Darwinism," Warren Avis et al.

"The Art of the Start: The Time-Tested, Battle-Hardened Guide for Anyone Starting Anything", Guy Kawasaki.

"Success Through A Positive Mental Attitude," Napoleon Hill and W Clement Stone.

Other Quotations websites:
http://www.minterest.com/99-inspirational-motivational-quotes-on-entrepreneurship/

http://work-at-home-based-business.com/2010/01/04/50-success-quotes-for-entrepreneurs/

http://businessnoob.com/26-inspirational-quotes-for-the-aspiring-entrepreneur/

Index

237

241

244

Failure is often the line of least persistence., 18

Failure is the opportunity, 70

Fall in love with your work, 150

Fallon, Ivan, 56

Fame is the spur, 204

Far better it is to dare mighty things, 16

Fate is what kicks you in the ass, 131

Faulkner, William, 135

Fearful unbelief in yourself, 183

Federal Express, 78

Feel needed. Feel useful. Feel good, 165

Feeling that they have been done down in some way, 192

Few men ever drop dead from overwork, 162

Few people take action to do so., 43

Feynman, Richard, 40, 195

Fidelity to a worthy purpose., 130

Fields, Debbie, 216

Fight to the finish, 167

Find a need and fill it!, 39

Firmly confident of victory, 166

Fitzgerald, Scott F., 64

Fitzgerlad, F. Scott, 122

Fleming, Sir Alexander Fleming, 125

Fly with the eagles, 169

Foch, Field Marshall, 123

Foch, Marshall, 74

Follow the talent to the dark place, 9

Forbes, B. C., 128

Forbes, Malcolm, 194, 222

Ford, Henry, 70, 89, 98, 116, 141, 166

Had to accept disappointments as their daily bread, 129

Hagen, Walter, 94

Hall, Tom T, 153

Hamel, Gary, 199, 212

Hammerskjold, Dag, 207

Happiness is that state of consciousness, 101

Happy is the man who, 194

Hard work, 57

Harris, Sidney J., 162

Hart, Rupert M., 118

Harvard Business School, 27, 38

Hatching the egg, 129

Hauser, Hermann, 3

Having eyes do you not see, 201

Hawthorne, Nathaniel, 158, 166

Hayakawa, S.I., 67

Hayward, Susan, 233

He conquers who endures, 165

He fails his talent, 12

He fills the room with his ideas, 51

He has achieved success, 32

He soars with his wings, 147

He that will not apply new remedies, 49

He wanted fame and fortune, 224

He wants his talents and work to be recognized, 170

He wants to leave a scratch on that wall, 135

He was a leader of leaders, 197

He was going to do something, 31

He who rides a tiger cannot dismount., 56

He wished to have joy and reason and meaning in life, 50

He's no failure, 116

Hegel, 162

Heinlein, Robert, 92

256

(Jack Burkhart is a pseudonym.)

www.ingramcontent.com/pod-product-compliance
Lightning Source LLC
Chambersburg PA
CBHW030254290526
45785CB00001B/77